D0983749

Eliminating Professors

The cover illustration entitled "Invalidation" is by
Honoré Daumier.

Eliminating Professors

A GUIDE TO THE DISMISSAL PROCESS

Kenneth Westhues

Professor of Sociology, University of Waterloo

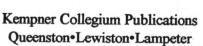

Kempner Collegium Publications
Queenston•Lewiston•Lampeter

The surname PITA, as used in this book, is an acronym. If a professor named Dr. PITA actually exists, he or she should not be confused with the character of the same name in this book.

**Eliminating Professors:
A Guide to the Dismissal Process**

ISBN 0-7734-8210-5

Kempner Collegium Publications

Published for the Robert Kempner Collegium by
The Edwin Mellen Press

For information contact

The Edwin Mellen Press	The Edwin Mellen Press
Box 67	Box 450
Queenston, Ontario	Lewiston, New York
CANADA L0S 1L0	USA 14092-0450

The Edwin Mellen Press, Ltd.
Lampeter, Ceredigion, Wales
UNITED KINGDOM SA48 8LT

Printed in the United States of America

Having confronted the story, we would much prefer to disbelieve, treating it as the product of a diseased mind, perhaps. And there are those today who ... are trying to persuade the world that the story is not true, urging us to treat it as the product of diseased minds, indeed. They are committing the greatest indignity human beings can inflict on one another, telling people who have suffered excruciating pain and loss that their pain and loss were illusions.

Robert McAfee Brown, preface to the 1986 edition of Elie Wiesel, *Night*.

Contents

Stage Four: Aftermath of the Incident

Stage Five: Elimination

Foreword

What prompted the research reported in this book was a phone call just after Labour Day in 1991, from a mathematics professor at the University of Waterloo. From reading my articles in the campus press, he thought I might be willing to help rectify a bizarre misunderstanding. A colleague of his, a renowned member of a renowned faculty, had been banned from teaching and dropped from the payroll on grounds that he had resigned, despite his claim that he had not resigned.

Thus began my study of the process by which people get eliminated from groups, organizations, and societies. Such study struck me as a sociologist's duty, to answer a public need. The professor who had allegedly resigned told me months later that when his troubles began, he had walked across campus to the sociology department, hoping somebody could give him an article or book that would shed light on his experience. I took the shedding of such light as a personal challenge. One after another, professors in process of elimination came to my attention. I pondered their cases, looking for common themes.

Then in the spring of 1994, my wife and colleague, Anne Westhues, passed on to me a report on Heinz Leymann's Scandinavian research on "workplace mobbing"—research that opened my eyes to the same essential process in nonacademic settings. Also that spring, I got the chance to study such a case in detail: the tortured story of a factory worker. Gradually I became aware that handling undesirables in the labour force is a major social problem—a fact confirmed in a recent multi-country survey done by the United Nations International Labour Organization.

While analyzing the problem in universities and other organizations, I also renewed my study of the literature on shunning, excommunication, and disfellowshipping in religious organizations, on blackballing in voluntary associations, on lynchings and witch hunts in communities, and on execution, imprisonment, and exile in national societies.

My generic term for the process comes from Daniel Goldhagen's 1996 book. Central to his argument is the concept of "eliminationist anti-Semitism," referring to a policy objective that Jews should cease to exist. Reading Goldhagen, I recalled what professors in my study had said to me: "I have become a non-person"; "They are trying to kill me"; "My life is finished." About this same time, a British academic administrator was in the news for admitting in a book that he sought to hasten the death of an undesirable colleague. By now, I have seen enough men and women physically and psychologically destroyed in their workplaces to conclude that *elimination* is not too strong a term, that applying this name to the general process does not demean but honours victims of the Holocaust, ethnic cleansing, and other instances of large-scale extermination. Little holocausts are happening every day in the workplaces of our most civilized societies.

At last, a sabbatical leave in the fall of 1997 brought an unexpected opportunity to set down practical applications of my six years of research in plain prose. Hence this book.

The specific focus here is on the five-stage process by which a university comes to define a professor as undesirable and then gets rid of him or her. This book is thus of most direct practical value to administrators, faculty members, and others in higher education.

Managers and officials concerned with human resource issues in other kinds of organization will find these chapters almost as useful, since I have included numerous references to nonacademic cases. Every corporation faces the problem of how to eliminate an employee with whom its contract is not simply at will, that is, dissolvable for any or no reason. Tenured professors are but an extreme example of employees who have a claim to permanence, often also seniority, autonomy, high salary, emotional ties and substantial investment of self. Employees of this kind are hard to terminate. Formally, they can be dismissed only for cause. The chapters here describe more common solutions.

Most basically, this book is about the mentalities, strategies, and stages involved in the elimination of anybody from any group. The expulsion of pariahs from a social circle—church, fraternity, college, factory, country—on which they depend for subsistence, respect, even life, is an awesome phenomenon. The eliminated are often shown to have been unworthy of membership from the start, never really to have belonged at all. The study of elimination beckons to scholars and citizens on all sides. Its subject matter is a basic human reality.

Even so, it is not something we like to think about, least of all in cases close to home. Like the fabled monkeys, we shield our eyes and ears from the event. We minimize how much we had to do with it: "My role was minor." We insist on its necessity: "Something had to be done." We chalk it up to natural causes: "His heart condition was bound to catch up with him sometime." We deny the event: "Beneath it all, I think she wasn't happy here and wanted to leave."

The beginning of wisdom is to face facts. Only then can we go on to study how facts connect. No one should take offense at the design of this book as a how-to guide for eliminating professors. Would you rather repress the hard facts of elimination and then, for want of careful planning, botch the job? Or perhaps carry on in blissful ignorance until you get eliminated yourself?

Little distinction is made here between moral and immoral instances of the process. In truth, the way you whack a good guy is identical to the way you whack a bad guy. A pillory fixes the neck of somebody in the right as securely as of somebody in the wrong. Just and unjust wars are waged with the same weapons, the same tactics, the same manoeuvres. No nation has ever, from its point of view, fought an unjust war. In the end, the victors feel relief and the vanquished feel pain. A chapter of this book quotes the vice-rector of a university in Rwanda: "Killing is a terrible thing, but in war people are killed. That is how it happens."

The war metaphor does not exactly fit. When a corporation is embattled against an employee, the sides are too poorly matched to call it war. There is too little doubt about who will win. The process analyzed in this book is less a cat fight than a cat-and-mouse game. The important point is that the conflict follows a pattern. Understanding the pattern is this book's aim.

"Whose Side Are We On?" Howard Becker asked in his 1966 presidential address to the Society for the Study of Social Problems. The side of the underdog, he proposed. In a rejoinder, Alvin Gouldner said no, we should be on the side of values that serve the public good.

Gouldner was right. As a Jewish boy, he might have read in the Torah:

> You must do no injustice in a case, neither showing partiality to the poor, nor deferring to the powerful, but judging your fellow fairly. ...
>
> You must not cherish hate against your fellow-countryman; you must be sure to reprove your fellow, but not incur sin because of him.

Eliminating Professors

Overview and Objective

The mortal choice which every German had to make—whether or not he knew he was making it—is a choice we Americans have never had to confront. But personal and professional life confronts us with the same kind of choice, less mortally, to be sure, every day.

Milton Mayer, *They Thought They Were Free*, 1955.

1

Carpe diem: September 28, 1997

The labour of this book begins tonight, though it is ten o'clock and I am tired. Anne, my wife, and I worked outside this Sunday afternoon, breathing in as perfect an autumn day as God could send. We enlarged a flower bed and moved some grape hyacinths into it. I trimmed the corkscrew hazel and tried to bring some Morrow honeysuckles into presentable shape.

All during the pruning and digging, even in the midst of small talk with my mate—we gardened together amicably today, unlike sometimes, when her plans and mine don't mesh—my mind was racing through the outline of this book. Then while she baked granola and an apple pie, I put the outline into my computer's memory. It is sure to change, but the basic thing is there.

For the next few weeks, the pause button of my life is likely to stay pushed, so I just as well use them to write a book that will be read.

For four years now, the academic administrators with authority over this particular professor's life have been taking steps toward getting rid of me. Not "with extreme prejudice" (as the CIA puts it), nor in the sense of curtailing my freedom as a citizen, nor even of destroying my career as a professor and sociologist. Their object, so far as I can tell, is merely to eliminate me from the department where I have worked these past 22 years.

3

The actions against me are numerous: a formal reprimand, restrictions on my teaching, findings of guilt on separate charges (one of sexism, more or less, and one of racism) by two different ethics tribunals, requirement of public apology, public condemnation in the university newspaper, refusal by the grievance panel to hear my case, official denunciation over the Internet, out-of-the-blue suspension without pay. Informally, the process began earlier. These past four years have been what I will call in later chapters "Stage Three" (the handling of an incident) and "Stage Four" (the aftermath of the handling of the incident), leading to the final stage, elimination.

Things now are at a turning point. This is not to say a finish line. The battle will probably go on as long as the parties to it still work at this university. The wounds from these past four years will stay open and raw as long as any of us lives. On account of the publicity, the scars will stay in the memory of this institution, and of Canadian academic life, long after all of us protagonists have died.

Even so, in a few weeks one or the other side of this dispute is probably going to take a hit. If it is me, I will lose a month's pay and step closer to the exit door. If it is the administrators, they will lose some credibility and I will try to go back to the professor's life I had before all this began. Now in this interlude, this time of awaiting a verdict but being too scared to guess what it will be, now is the time to write this book. A few weeks from now I will be too eager to move on.

Last June 11, the president of the university decided at long last to get me off his desk. I suppose the conflicting pressures had become too great. On one side my department chair, the provost, and public opinion generally among the campus who's who. On the other side the Canadian Association of University Teachers (CAUT), the Canadian Civil Liberties Association (CCLA), the Academic Freedom and Tenure Committee of the Faculty

Association of the University of Waterloo (FAUW), and possibly most worrisome the prospect of adverse public opinion outside the university.

The president did not admit to being on the hot seat. "You refer to my involvement in earlier matters as well as my letter dated March 20, 1997. I do not accept that these matters would preclude me from properly dealing with an appeal under Policy 33. I am anxious, however, to ensure that the appeal is dealt with expeditiously and I see no value in a prolonged argument on this issue." Translation: this is a no-win predicament, and I'm bailing out. Nobody had threatened a prolonged argument.

The president unloaded this particular trouble, among the many cluttering his desk, onto a colleague at a neighbouring university: the former dean of its law school now its "vice-president (administration) and general counsel." Receive submissions from Westhues on all the matters he raises, the president wrote to him, and provide your written decision no later than the first of August. Conduct your investigation by whatever procedures you choose. I "undertake to be bound by your determination of the appeal as if it were my own." That is what the president wrote.

It was mid-July before this Outside Judge contacted me. I liked him—which means very little because I like most people. He decided that the two parties to this dispute are the provost and me, and so set up a kind of hearing on August 7. He said he wanted just the three of us to be there, along with a tape recorder. I said any location was okay with me except for our administration building, the one the provost works in.

The hearing was set for 9:00 AM in Room 123 of Hagey Hall of the Humanities (it sounds best in cockney). The provost and I arrived first, a good ten minutes before the Outside Judge. It was a sparkling summer day, the kind you hate to waste sitting in a windowless seminar room with brown brick walls. I brought coffee

for the three of us from Tim Horton's. I figured caffeine might
ease tensions, and I wasn't sure the coffee shop near Hagey Hall
would be open, on account of summer holidays.

The provost is the cigarette man—so he was described last
year in a math professor's parody on *X-files*. I smoke, too. That
gave us something to make jokes about. The Outside Judge said
he didn't normally smoke, but he would on this occasion, so we
took a smoke break outside. He wanted to bum a cigarette but I
worried about giving him one. Years ago I acceded to a normally
non-smoking colleague's request for a cigarette, and he passed
out.

The provost gave the Outside Judge his first cigarette, and
thankfully the Judge did not pass out. On our second break I said
that to show impartiality, the Outside Judge would have to accept
a cigarette from me, and that just as after the provost's cigarette,
he would not be allowed to pass out. He agreed, body and soul.

While the three of us were standing outside the building on
our second smoke break, a colleague from history came walking
by and joked that we looked like a conspiracy. Heh, I thought, if
he only knew! Protestations to the contrary notwithstanding, the
provost was trying to rid the university of one sociology professor.
If he should fail (Lady Macbeth: "We fail!"), his own
administrative authority would be weakened. How could we stand
there joking and blowing smoke when the stakes were so high? A
strange place, the university: nowhere else are operations so
covert. That is because nowhere else is a value on speaking
openly so enshrined.

For three hours we met, or had the hearing, or whatever it
was we did. The Outside Judge said he would send a transcript
with his decision. I hope the printed version captures our good
humour. None of us said a single harsh word. Well, I guess there
was one. The provost said I was mean. I said that was beside the
point.

Since our hearing took place on August 7, the Outside Judge was obviously not going to meet the president's deadline of August 1. He said he had vacation coming up, and would work on his decision during it. (Not surprising: professors do that sort of thing. Lazy we are not. Misguided maybe, but we work at it.) He said he would provide us with his decision in three weeks.

To make it as an academic administrator, you treat decisions like this the way a surgeon supposedly treats a decision some patient's life is hanging on. You keep your heart out of it, or pretend to. It's a judgment call, detached and dispassionate, fascinating from an analytic point of view. All the world's a case, an instance of a rule. For the person who *is* the case, the pretense is harder to maintain. I did my best.

On August 29, I telephoned the Outside Judge's secretary. She professed not to know anything about the matter. Did I want him to phone me? I said no, that it is against the rules in a dispute like this for one party to contact the adjudicator privately. Would she please ask him, if the report was to be substantially delayed, to let the provost and me know.

"Gentlemen," so read the fax that came on September 2, addressed to the provost and me. "I expect to send my decision with reasons at the beginning of next week. I regret the delay but I did not have as much vacation time to myself as I had expected when we last spoke. Thanks for your patience."

Was that a good sign or a bad one? (When you are a professor-to-be-gotten-rid-of, you occupy yourself trying to pick up subtle cues, likely a waste of time.) Was the Outside Judge demonstrating his sensitivity to due process or was he accommodating my concern on the small matter of timing while preparing to reinforce my outlaw status in the substance of his report?

I do not yet know, because he did not meet his new deadline either. Later in this book I will have more to say about deadlines.

Deadlines

Handling them adroitly is crucial to success in achieving the
objective with which this book is concerned.

I might as well have spent the first three weeks of September
golfing (which tops my list of unproductive activities), for all the
work I got done. Morning, noon and night, the Outside Judge's
impending verdict was on my mind, the more so because it was
not in my mailbox. Being made to wait is a form of torture. It can
break the toughest mind. It does not get easier with practice.

On September 18, I faxed the Outside Judge (copy to the
provost) a polite little note inquiring if his decision was further
delayed, or whether perhaps it was misdirected in the mail. No
answer came.

My patience was lost by three days ago, September 25. I
cannot recall any time during these past four years when irritation
so overwhelmed me. I drafted a letter to the Outside Judge.
Maybe I should have run it by my mate. She is a professor, too.
She has often saved me from an imprudent missive. I didn't want
her to save me from this one. Besides, this struggle weighs her
down as much as me. You know that song, "What do you get
when you fall in love?" I'm afraid to ask how often she sings it to
herself.

"Just as I have earlier asked administrative officers and
committees here to abide by university policy, so now I ask you
to abide by the terms of reference of your appointment.

"From your first telephone call to me on 8 July, up to and
including your fax to the provost and me on 2 September, I had
the impression that even if behind schedule, your handling of the
task entrusted to you was correct, attentive, and above-board. All
you need to do to maintain that impression is fax the provost and
me a brief reply to my inquiry of 18 September, a further copy of
which I send herewith. With thanks and good wishes, Sincerely."

We were just turning in at eleven o'clock that night (our
high-schooler son gets up early for class this term, hence our

hours are less owlish than usual) when a fax arrived from the Outside Judge.

"I apologize for not responding to your fax of September 18. I was out of the country from September 17 to 22 and have not yet reviewed the correspondence I received during that time. I am also sorry not to have sent my decision by this time. I won't bore you with the list of administrative woes that have intruded except to say that a retreat from Friday through Saturday and a negotiation planning meeting on Sunday will all but ruin this weekend as well.

"That said, I am still aiming to get my decision to you by the end of next week. Sincerely."

I put the odds of his decision reaching me by this coming Friday at 20 percent, by two weeks from now at 40 percent, and steadily higher for the next four weeks. After that the odds go up that his decision will not arrive at all, that the Outside Judge will discover a conflict of interest and leave for a sabbatical in Zanzibar. The longer his decision is delayed, the greater the likelihood, too, that the president here will come up with a reason to cancel this exercise. The best reason would be some compelling new charges to bring against me, grave enough to justify formal dismissal.

How then shall I spend these next few weeks? I am supposed to be on a sabbatical leave until the first of the year: a time, according to academic folklore, for peaceful reflection, reading, and writing.

I have tried to make the folklore come true. My first intellectual love, thirty odd years ago when I was still an undergraduate, was the history of the Boonslick region of Missouri, where I was born and grew up. It had been settled by Southern planters and slaves in the 1830s, and by the time of the Civil War was the northwesternmost outpost of the culture of the South. German immigrants like my father's parents later moved in and replaced the glamor of aristocracy with mundane democratic work. My first book, way back in 1966, was on Boonslick history.

These past few weeks I have tried to plunge into that history again, with a view maybe to revising that first, sophomoric book. Take your mind out of this century, I told myself, out of the university, out of Waterloo, Ontario, and Canada. Make a Zanzibar in your mind and go there. Better that than worrying yourself to death.

The design has not worked. Data from nineteenth-century Boonslick are spread across my desk, but my mind will not focus on them. Bloom where you're planted, isn't that good advice?

Carpe diem, so reads a mug my mate gave me. When you pour hot coffee in, the English appears: *Seize the Day*. Why not seize these next few weeks to give administrators practical advice about how to get rid of undesirables like me? Ninety years ago, in the face of contradiction and paradox, William James felt "duty bound to unravel and explain it," because he was "a professor drawing a full salary." For the same reason, the same duty now falls on me.

Let me not be coy. This book is not arriving by stork. For years now, since long before my own troubles began, I have gathered clippings, chatted with colleagues, scribbled notes, and read books about the processes by which professors here at Waterloo and elsewhere have been removed from jobs supposedly secure. Now is the time to pull these notes together and offer something useful to the people governing our universities.

The basis on which I write is not just these past four years, when I have been on the wrong side of administrative power. I had been on the right side for two decades before that. For three years, 1975 to 1978, I was the widely praised chair of the sociology department here. The dean said the vote was unanimous that I continue in that job.

I have looked at the cloud of professorial undesirability from both sides. I have gazed upon it, too, as an outsider in the universities elsewhere in Canada, the United States, and Europe where I have spent time as a visiting professor. This book is based on analysis of about 25 undesirables besides myself. The angles from which I have inspected them vary from one to the next.

Enough introduction! On to the substance of the book! I do not know how much time I have before the Outside Judge will end this precious interlude in my biography, the necessary condition for formulating what is written here.

2

Readership

No author can specify a book's readership. Once the book is in print, there is no telling who may pick it up, read it, and make use of it. The *Communist Manifesto* has been read by many times more middle-class students than by the workers of the world to whom Marx and Engels directed it. The diary Anne Frank wrote just for herself has been read by millions on every continent.

Even so, every author should let readers know to whom the word *you* refers. This is because every author has some prospective category of reader in mind. The author tries to step into those imagined readers' shoes and say things that will interest them. If readers walking in shoes of a different size and shape also take an interest, well, that cannot be helped and may be all to the good.

In this book, *you* refers to a set of people whose jobs have a special heaviness: line administrators in today's universities. On the front lines you are chairs of departments in academic fields like physics or philosophy, and directors or deans of professional schools, as in architecture or accounting. For you, administering is a part-time add-on to teaching and research.

At the next level up, you are faculty deans, with authority over some grouping of academic departments and professional schools. For you, academic administration is a full-time job.

Perhaps you are the Graduate Dean, a key role in most universities.

At the top level you are the president, provost, academic vice-president, or someone assisting them (usually with the title of *associate* this or that) in administering the institution as a whole. You are part of the central administration or, in current parlance, senior management.

This book is for academic administrators at all these levels. You have a hard row to hoe. You are supposed to bring order to the work of unruly minds. You must preside over tenured professors who—so it often seems—have more autonomy than you have authority. Your carrots are puny and your sticks break. You have to balance the books of an organization whose key workers claim to be above mundane financial cares—except that each demands a raise bigger than the next.

You get less respect than you deserve. You came to your position through the will of a committee composed mainly of people who are now formally your subordinates. Do they act like it? They resist the very word *employee*, treating you sometimes as a beast of burden on whom to unload their responsibilities.

Nor are you especially well-paid, relative to those for whom you make excuses. Your salary is probably that of any other professor, except that you get an annual stipend of five or ten thousand dollars more. In a business, the spread between you and your subordinates would likely be greater. No wonder they show you so little respect.

Maybe you are the president. You earn $150,000 or $200,000 a year, and suffer the indignity of having the exact amount published in the newspaper. For every one day in the sunshine of spring convocation there are ten in thunderclouds of paperwork. Worst of all, you can see in lots of professors' eyes that they hold you in disdain. You wonder how many of them nurse the ingratitude of Harvard economist John Kenneth Galbraith:

American university presidents are a nervous breed; I have never thought well of them as a class. ... They are paid above scale to suffer for the free expression of the less convenient members of the faculty but rarely believe they should have to earn their pay.

So what if you are not a president, but only a department chair or dean? Your professors are not Galbraiths either. Too many of them share his sentiments.

I do not know why you hold your administrative job. Maybe you don't either. Motivations vary. But if you are a serious administrator, you would really like to bring some order to the haphazard, conflicting, ambiguous, chaotic scene surrounding you. You feel in the marrow of your bones the need to rationalize the academic workplace. The times insist on it. Budgets are tight. Governments want accountability. Stakeholders demand a say. The media relish exposing academic waste.

You know that in the competitive global economy, universities cannot continue as in past centuries. Every academic unit needs to pay its own way. Objectives have to be spelled out, and performance indicators implemented for measuring progress toward goals. Inefficiencies have to be corrected. Downsizing may be required. Playful reflection is a luxury in these straightened economic times. Academic programs that cannot deliver goods with some tangible payoff will have to be rethought.

In sum, you know as an academic administrator that the future of your institution lies in careful planning, streamlining, and rationalization. Your job is to manage the process in your corner of the academic world. You aim to do your job well. My purpose in this book is to assist you with sound technical advice for a problem that may already have devoured weeks of your time and energy.

3

The problem of Dr. PITA

The administrative problem this book is designed to help you with can best be described with a personal name: Dr. PITA. He may be a he. She may be a she. There is no telling what the subject's age, race, marital status, field of study, or politics may be. The one thing sure is that PITA is a Pain In The Ass. Hence the name. Apologies to anyone who actually has it.

Tenure makes PITA who and what she is. If PITA's appointment were of a sessional, visiting, temporary, or definite-term variety, as defined by university policy, PITA would not be a pita. PITA would be gone.

But PITA has tenure—or a similar kind of continuing status that prevents him from being summarily fired.

The problem with which this book is concerned is how to eliminate Dr. PITA. I do not mean how to get rid of undesirable professors generally. That will be a long, slow process, involving countless battles in newspapers, university senates, legislatures and courts toward the end of abolishing tenure as a condition of any professor's employment.

The problem that is our focus here is the immediate one you have with that flesh-and-blood embodiment of undesirability named PITA, who currently inhabits the academic unit for which you have responsibility. I know this is not the name on his office door. None of the 25 professors I have studied as the basis for

15

this book is (or was) listed in the calendar as Dr. PITA. Neither is the professor you are thinking of. No matter. Dr. PITA is really a single being, a destructive force operating under varied names.

An administrator whose life was consumed by Dr. PITA for some years wrote me these comments on an essay of mine about current issues in universities: "In my experience, there are some academics who are organizationally difficult people (perhaps because of personal characteristics) whose difficulties at base have little to do with the sorts of academic issues you discuss but which tend to become elaborated in an academic rationale. The personal characteristics precipitate all sorts of difficulties of human relationships in areas which have an academic content, but the real issue may not be the academic content but the difficulty and the personal characteristics which precipitate it.

"Such individuals may become expert in manipulating due process in order to defend themselves on issue after issue. Informal discussion with university administrators contains scuttlebutt about how every university has a couple of types like those who are 'troublemakers' who know how to go just so far and no farther, and who create a fear in administrators of taking them on because of the endless hours required by due process."

Dear administrator, with the present book in hand you need never fearaking   Dr. PITA on. You already know that the problem resides not in any attributes of the organization you are managing but in her, in the personal characteristics that make her who she is. The problem is how to get rid of her—him, it, that.

4

The objective: PITA's elimination

What you need to do is apply to the PITA problem the same principles of rational planning with which you approach questions of budget, enrollment, and curriculum. First you formulate your objective explicitly. Then you detail a step-by-step plan for achieving it in a defined time-frame. Finally you implement the plan, assessing progress toward the objective at each step along the way.

You may feel initial discomfort at applying these principles to this human-resource issue. In the traditional conception of a university, tenure implied a lifelong or career-long moral commitment between colleagues, an imagined bond of reciprocal trust. Each was expected to tolerate the other's rants and ravings, no matter how unsound, unbalanced, unmarketable, or unpopular.

To the extent that this traditional mentality lingers in you, you may feel guilt at planning PITA's elimination. You may be reluctant to admit even to yourself what your objective is. To that extent, your effectiveness will be reduced. Haphazard, half-hearted efforts are no way to achieve anything.

A century ago, marriage was commonly understood to be a lifelong moral commitment. Couples stayed together in misery, feeling guilt at the thought of divorce. The challenge you face now, as an academic manager open to innovation and change, is

to apply the same enlightened mentality to academic life as is now
commonly applied to married life. Your goal is to divorce PITA
from your academic unit, a unit whose integrity he undermines.

If the traditional conception of tenure still lingers inside
you, despite your position of leadership, it is probably accepted
without question by many of your colleagues. Besides, many of
them may fail to appreciate what a festering sore upon the
academic body Dr. PITA is, and may have formed emotional ties
to him. It is therefore crucial that you not publicly acknowledge
the objective you are pursuing in the PITA case, and if necessary
deny that you have ever thought of it, at the same time keeping
clearly in mind your plan for achieving it.

Remind yourself also of the limits of your authority. You
are not a judge in a public court. Your authority does not extend
to putting PITA in jail or depriving her of the rights and freedoms
all citizens enjoy in a free society. Your authority is over one
workplace: a university or some part thereof. That workplace is
a tiny corner of the world in which PITA can go about her life. If
she has foolishly invested a great deal of herself in this
educational system, while at the same time being sand in its gears,
that is her problem, not yours.

Once you have formulated explicitly the objective of
removal in the PITA case and committed yourself to achieving it,
you will immediately see that it is not at all out of reach. Even
granting the security tenure implies in academic custom and
university policies, there are at least ten alternative exit doors
through which Dr. PITA can eventually be pushed. Each of these
doors has been used successfully in at least one case in my survey.

As you read through the list, mentally check off the ones
that seem handiest in the case that weighs on you.

- **Resignation.** Dr. PITA may take your initial hints and leave
  voluntarily for another job. This is the single best way your
  objective can be achieved: it costs you nothing and everybody

smiles. You can arrange a going-away party and lead the chorus of colleagues wishing PITA success in her new endeavour. Regrettably, she may not be marketable. She may not want to move. Because PITA is a pita, she may prefer to fight than switch.

- **Fabricated resignation.** If Dr. PITA will not resign, it may be possible to pretend that he has and make the pretense stick. Any written statement from him that includes the words *I resign* or *It's all over* or *I've had enough* can be seized. An absence from campus taken without your written authorization may be amenable to interpretation as legal abandonment of his position.
- **Transfer.** This is not an option if your institution is small, and if you are a president who has to contend with PITA no matter what corner of the university she is in, this is not really an exit-door. If you are a department chair or dean, however, transfer to an academic unit on the far side of campus may get PITA out of your hair and budget just as completely as if she dropped dead.
- **Death.** Like quitting, this exit-door entails no cost to your institution. It should never be ruled out. The criminal code forbids direct efforts on your part to push PITA through this door, and in most of America, murder is a capital offense. Yet by increasing the level of PITA's work-related stress, you improve the odds that he will succumb to a stress-related illness like heart attack or stroke. Alternatively, he may take his own life. By staying constantly "on his case," you lower the ability of PITA's immune system to resist disease.
- **Long-term disability, physical illness.** The same administrative hassling that raises the odds of PITA taking the exit just described, raises the odds for this one, too. Your university's insurance plan will keep him out of your hair for two years or more, if he is shown to be totally incapable of doing a

professor's normal work. After two years away from campus, PITA will be older, less confident, behind in his research, and even if he returns to work, less able to be a pita than before.

- **Long-term disability, mental illness.** Everything said about physical disability applies equally to mental disability. But this is an exit-door through which he can more easily be pushed. To put it crudely, you simply drive PITA mad—before he drives you mad. The university's psychiatrist knows how stressful academic life can be, and will undoubtedly be attentive to any concerns you care to express about PITA's mental health.

- **Early retirement.** Your university surely has a practice, if not a public plan, to sweeten the termination package of undesirable professors who are willing to depart after 55 but before the normal retirement age. If you are a department chair, discuss this option with your dean, who may grumble a bit. Explain how disruptive PITA is. Emphasize how the cost of an early-retirement package is offset by hiring PITA's replacement at the junior level. As for PITA himself, if you have made his life difficult enough, health problems may make him eager to take whatever settlement you, as a friend, can obtain for him.

- **Dismissal for cause.** Forget about dismissing Dr. PITA on grounds that her teaching or research is substandard. In these postmodern times, she will almost surely produce experts to testify that her scholarship, however whacko it may be, is on the cutting edge. You, meanwhile, become an object of public ridicule, as an enemy of academic freedom. If your objective is not met by one of the options preceding, search for some ethical ground on which to bring a dismissal case. Later chapters describe procedures for doing this.

- **Downsizing or financial exigency.** The policies of your university undoubtedly provide that a tenured professor can be let go if, in the face of a budget crunch, the program he or she is working in is discontinued. To push Dr. PITA through this exit-door may require extensive preliminary planning: isolating him in the program destined for oblivion, juggling figures to demonstrate the program's unsustainability, and then implementing the relevant policy. This process may take several years, but it has a proven record of success in certain cases.

- **Constructive dismissal.** With sufficient provocation of the kinds suggested in later chapters, you will find Dr. PITA shouting one day in your office, "I'm going to sue." This should be music to your ears. With luck, he will quit and sue for constructive dismissal, claiming that you made his life unbearable. The university's legal team will tie him up in technicalities for months and bleed him dry. After remortgaging his house to pay his lawyer, PITA will probably be glad to settle out of court. If he should win in court, he will not be reinstated but only awarded monetary damages, typically in Canada a month's salary for every year he was employed—quite a modest price to pay for getting rid of him. This exit-door should be used with caution in the United States, since American law allows juries to award more generous damages.

    Don't you feel better already? Your hands are not so tied as an unsophisticated reading of the tenure policy may make it seem. You do not have to take the scourge of Dr. PITA lying down. At least ten different doors are available through which he can exit your department, faculty or university, and thereby contribute to its smoother functioning. All Dr. PITA needs is some help from you.

5

Marks of undesirability

Before outlining stages and strategies in the process of Dr. PITA's elimination, a few pages of description are in order, for the sake of identifying him.

In all likelihood, he does not look bad on paper—a fact that makes his presence the more insidious. He may have a considerable student following, though he is more likely to appeal strongly to a minority of students than mildly to the majority. Comments on student course evaluations bring to light PITA's tendency to raise more questions than he answers, to speak on the authority of research outside the consensus of his peers in the academic unit, and to display a certain disdain or irreverence toward administrators. Being young and impressionable, some students relish PITA's teaching, enough that the numerical scores on his evaluations are probably at or above the faculty average.

Dr. PITA is probably also active in research, the number of her publications being equal or above the number for her colleagues. This reflects the fact that she works hard, to the point that her scholarly undertakings have become a consuming passion. She is ill-adept at separating her professional from her personal life, and is likely to bring a sense of calling or vocation to her work. The result is a rate of research productivity that makes her seem, from her printed *resumé* or *vita*, the kind of professor most universities would find desirable.

Usually, however, Dr. PITA displays an intense commitment to ideas that are contrary to the basic principles ingrained in the department, faculty or university. Because the foundational principles vary from one academic setting to the next, so, too, do the discordant ideas Dr. PITA puts forward—and comes back to at every opportunity. Following are some of the dissident positions taken by Dr. PITA in the cases in my study, positions that became bones of contention as the process of elimination was played out:

- That psychological learning disabilities are for the most part mere excuses for low achievement.
- That students should be allowed to drop a course without penalty right up to the end of the semester.
- That social-science professors should rely less on expert opinion and more on the wisdom of everyday people.
- That most administrators in the university have forgotten the difference between truth and lies.
- That the department's degree programs are in urgent need of external assessment and reform.
- That women and members of visible minorities should not be given preferential treatment in academic life.
- That the canon in most humanistic fields is biased toward dead white males.
- That racial differences in IQ are real, and should inform public-policy debates.
- That social research is best conducted ethnographically, as opposed to quantitatively and statistically.
- That social research is best conducted quantitatively and statistically, as opposed to ethnographically.
- That professors should not profit financially from results of research paid for with public funds.

Even from this short list, you can see that no particular teaching makes Dr. PITA who he is. It is the clash between his teaching and that of the professors with whom he shares academic space that is often a key feature of his identity. This is especially likely if he refuses to keep his teaching strictly academic and insists on "doing something about it"—that is, trying to bend policy and administrative decisions to his views.

Dr. PITA is a different type than the harmless, often charming posturers that commonly walk academic corridors. I mean professors who enjoy playing devil's advocate, voicing outrageous hypotheses, or expending eloquence on high ideals whose impracticality they nonetheless recognize. Academics of this kind may be annoying at times, but they can be counted on, having said their piece, to acquiesce to the collegial consensus. Their views are tolerated because everybody knows these are things they have to say but do not expect anyone to act upon. Dr. PITA, by contrast, is not joking. She expects her views to be taken seriously, no matter how far outside the consensus they lie. If she had her way, things would have to change.

Jon Dellandrea, vice-president of the University of Toronto, made the point tellingly a decade ago, when he was vice-president at the University of Waterloo. Referring to Albert Einstein, he told a reporter that "old Albert" would not belong on Waterloo's faculty, on account of his unconcern with marketable scholarship. In the context of Waterloo, this is to say, Einstein would be Dr. PITA, a scholar too smart for his own good, to whom you, as a line manager, would responsibly apply the objective set forth in the title of this book.

On the other hand, in many of Dr. PITA's incarnations, her teaching does not pose a serious threat to the established academic wisdom, and an observer may at first be puzzled as to why she is intolerable. The puzzle is solved by recognizing that professors in universities are not just intellects but whole human beings who crave the company of people like themselves as assurance of their self-worth. Anyone who "stands out from the crowd" in any way except to excel in what the group values most is a menace to it.

Your pita, like most of those in my study, is probably not world-renowned for anything. He is a lesser light shining in the wrong direction and casting a shadow over everybody else. That he does not fit may be signalled by attributes as trivial as these:

- A mode of dress, speech, address, or deportment that mocks the norms other people take for granted;
- An asymmetrical or odd facial appearance, a tic or stutter, that drags down the public image of the group;
- A foreign accent, publication in foreign journals, or similar signs of compromised allegiance;
- A place of residence, political ties, or associations off-campus that flout what your academic unit stands for; or
- The exercise of talent in a way that benefits an outside group, in effect snubbing the academic employer.

Still, whatever the dimensions of PITA's difference from his colleagues, what makes *different* in his case a synonymn for *undesirable*? What makes PITA's quirkiness intolerable, while other professors' quirks are overlooked?

Somehow, PITA is threatening. She is not pathetic, in the sense of arousing the pity of her colleagues. She is too bold to be pitied, too much of a menace to be regarded with silent contempt and allowed to fumble her way unmolested to the oblivion that awaits. One effect of the elimination process may be to turn PITA into a pathetic figure, but she is not that yet.

Nor can PITA be classed with the dead wood of which most universities have a fair supply. He is toxic in his aliveness. If he would lie still in a corner and not make noise, his presence might be bearable, but he does not. He pokes around where he does not belong and expects rewards for it.

The question is not really what makes Dr. PITA insufferable, but who makes him so, and the answer is you. The head knows best what the body is about. In choosing you for leadership of your department or faculty, or of the university itself, the institution has acknowledged your grasp of its basic principles, the elusive and intangible norms that define its character. Further, you accepted the appointment out of sincere commitment to preserving and strengthening that institutional character. If a professor under your authority rankles your very soul—gets under your skin, as the saying goes—it must be because that professor is a danger to the group you represent.

W. I. Thomas, a sociology professor who was dismissed for cause in 1918 from his tenured position at the University of Chicago, wrote an insight still quoted in textbooks: "If men define a situation as real, it is real in its consequences." If your gut tells you, as an administrator, that one of your professors is Dr. PITA in disguise, he really is Dr. PITA, and you are compelled to try to make this fact real in its consequences. Coming chapters tell you how to do it.

Two Initial Stages:

Ostracization and Harassment

The bystander effect is watching some evil take place, but since we are watching with others who are watching, and no one seems to be doing anything about the evil, we go on watching and doing nothing about it.

Carol Bly, *Changing the Bully Who Rules the World*, 1996, in the chapter entitled, "Evil in the Comfortable Herd."

6

Marking PITA out

The first stage in the process of PITA's elimination involves identifying him informally, marking him out as a professor who does not belong. This stage, whose duration may range from months to years, is subtle, covert, sometimes almost imperceptible. If challenged, you easily deny that any exclusionary process is afoot. Yet this stage is the essential prerequisite to later ones.

Success requires keen awareness on your part that you cannot get rid of PITA singlehandedly. You need the support of your superiors and subordinates in the administrative hierarchy. You also need to be able to count on some number of rank-and-file professors, given the priority on collegial decision-making in academic politics. Under no circumstances should you proceed without assurance of the requisite support. Doing so could make you look foolish and cost you your administrative job.

Actually, it is more than a matter of garnering support. To the extent that people get the idea that you "have it in for Sam" or are "out to get Susie," your cause is lost. You must not allow the situation to be defined as rivalry, a personality clash, or intellectual disagreement between you and PITA. Such a definition would place you and him on an equal footing, and invite colleagues either to stay out of the fray or take sides with one of you. As one individual at war with another, you might lose.

What you need to do in your leadership role is make PITA's elimination a truly collective process. You need to create and cultivate a dynamic in your academic unit that leaves PITA out, and then surrender yourself to that dynamic. In this way, as your actions against PITA become in due course more overt, others will see you not as pursuing a private crusade or personal vendetta, but instead as acting on their behalf, in the interests of the group. You and those you lead need to be captives of one another.

By no means should you take the initial steps yourself. Let PITA take them for you. She will rankle lots of people by pressing her aberrant views or flaunting her strange mannerisms. In one case after another in my study, people have said of PITA, "She is her own worst enemy." She doesn't know when to shut up. If she is true to her name, she will put more and more people off—the same people with whom you are in solidarity. In truth, it is not a matter of you "going after her." It is a matter of her positioning herself steadily farther outside the steadily stronger consensus over which you preside.

There are four main indicators that this stage is proceeding as it should. First, PITA does not get elected to key committees on appointments, promotion, tenure, performance review, academic planning or curriculum, nor onto faculty executive committees or the university senate. This means his colleagues do not consider him the sort of professor to whom they want to entrust decisions important to their working lives. It also means PITA is outside the main networks of collegial friendship, and is probably spending little time working rooms and amassing social capital. Perhaps by now, PITA says he has better things to do than sit on committees anyway.

Second, PITA is in the losing minority on crucial votes in faculty meetings. If your academic unit is the kind where PITA's elimination can be most easily accomplished, most decisions made at such meetings enjoy near-unanimous support. It matters little what the votes are about. The important thing is that the bulk of participants are of one mind, while PITA is of a different mind.

Third, nobody much responds, unless in a curt, dismissive way, to PITA's interventions at faculty meetings, colloquia, seminars or as letters to the editor in the campus newspaper. In the view of the silent majority, PITA is just spouting off again, from outside the circle of relevant conversation. She seems not to be tuned in to what everybody else is saying. Frustrated at being ignored, PITA's voice may become strident: "Will somebody please answer me!" If you are chairing the gathering, you are careful not to take the bait. By engaging her in argument, you would lower yourself to her level, bolster her credibility, and place your own leadership at risk.

Fourth and most important, mention of PITA's name when colleagues gather in the lunch room, at the photocopy machine or in the corridors calls forth witticisms that symbolically separate him from desirable company. An archetypal example was a quick word I was having years ago with an administrator engaged, until then unbeknownst to me, in the process of eliminating a foreign-accented pita. The professor's name came up in passing and the administrator mimicked the accent so briefly she could have denied having done so if I had rebuked her for it. Then she looked at me, grinned, and picked up on our conversation as if no joke had been made.

From these four indicators it is plain that PITA's elimination is and must be a general social process. In the initial stage it is wholly informal, a gradual isolation of Dr. PITA from the ongoing life of the academic unit. Your task at this stage is mainly the positive, constructive one of forging a strong sense of unity around your department's, faculty's, or university's overall mission, and the programs and policies necessary for fulfilling it. That Dr. PITA is not a team player will be recognized more and more as time goes on, without your doing anything explicit to bring this about.

Now and again you can test the waters by making to a fellow administrator or subordinate the kind of joke the administrator made to me. You can roll your eyes for a moment when somebody tells you of PITA's latest indiscretion. Take note of the response you get. If it is a blank or unapproving stare, back off quickly. You cannot afford to be seen as PITA's enemy. If, on the other hand, the response is a slight smile, be encouraged. Shared humour of this kind, even if no words are exchanged, is a secret pact of common cause, that you can draw upon in due course.

7

Techniques of torment

By keeping your ear to the ground of the academic unit for which you are responsible, you know how far the first stage has progressed, the stage of Dr. PITA's identification as a misfit. At some point his apartness from everybody else will be obvious enough that professors will comment on it discreetly in conversations with you. A department chair considered that a corner had been turned when a colleague remarked in an anguished voice, "It's a pity, you know, so much of what Sam says is true, but for the good of the department, he must be isolated."

The turning of that corner opens the way for the second stage in the process of PITA's elimination, a stage in which you exercise your authority creatively to nudge him further toward the exit-doors. Often, of course, Stages One and Two proceed apace, the latter at a slight time-lag. The important point is that you should take a proactive role only after a supportive climate is in place. You begin to take action against Dr. PITA only with the tacit permission of your subordinates—or perhaps with their informal encouragement.

While it is true that as an academic executive, you lack as much power over tenured faculty as your counterparts in business have over their subordinates, you should not underestimate the power you do have. A wise senior colleague in my early years of teaching used to say, "The way to get power is to seize it."

If you are a front-line admnistrator, you probably have sole or shared discretion over the following critical aspects of Dr. PITA's working life:

- How large a salary increase, if any, he gets each year;
- The written evaluation of his work in the annual performance review;
- The assignment of his physical office, possibly also lab space and parking spot;
- The assignment of which courses he should teach;
- The scheduling of his courses as to day and time of day;
- Which administrative chores and committees he should be assigned to;
- How soon, if at all, he should be promoted to the rank of associate or full professor;
- Whether to nominate him for internal grants and awards;
- Approval of his expense claims for travel, research assistance, computer time, and so on;
- Provision of teaching assistance or help with marking;
- The timing, if not the award, of his next sabbatical;
- Forwarding with your recommendation his applications for research grants;
- Any unusual requests he makes for exceptions to normal practice—a course remission one term, for example, in return for teaching an extra course the following term.

If you are a higher-level administrator, only some of these areas of decision require your signature, but they are the ones that most seriously affect Dr. PITA's career.

In decades past, when universities could afford to be run more loosely, administrators were accustomed to rubber-stamping most faculty requests. It was often easier to let undesirable professors have their way than fight with them. It still is easier, in the case of professors who are in tune with the overall objectives of your academic unit.

In these tough times, however, no rational purpose is served by accommodating and facilitating the requests of a professor who stands outside and against the group. Neither pity nor a misguided sense of fairness should distract you from your organizational responsibility to frustrate PITA's working life in every way consistent with established policy, and thereby hasten his departure.

You should not violate policy or deny approvals or perks to which PITA is clearly entitled. If you do, your decision may be overruled. Hard-won progress toward your objective may be lost. Neither should you admit to what you are doing, even to fellow administrators, much less to PITA's peers. Always listen to her with a straight face and show courtesy. Meanwhile keep in your desk a store of red tape and pull it out each time PITA seeks your support:

- Delay your signature on routine documents on account of being out of town or tied up in meetings;
- Sit on matters to which PITA attaches great urgency;
- Miss deadlines PITA needs you to keep;
- Request additional receipts or documentation before sending PITA's forms through the pipe, as a favour to her, to prevent questions being raised by higher-ups;
- Refer PITA's requests to a committee for discussion and recommendation before giving your decision;
- Insist on a strict deadline for anything PITA has to do;
- Say you need to consult with your superiors before taking action on PITA's requests.

The second stage of PITA's elimination is essentially a series of messages you send, reminding him that his presence in the academic unit is no longer valued. Routine administration affords many opportunities to send such messages, once you look for them. Here are two real-life examples (I have changed the identifying details.)

Dr. PITA had published analyses of conflict in Israel, and was partisan to the Palestinian cause. He succeeded over much opposition in introducing a course entitled "Middle Eastern Politics," and taught it with obvious relish. Several respected members of the department confided to the chair that they thought PITA's approach to the topic biased. Indeed, they suspected he was an anti-Semite. For the next academic year, the chair asked PITA to teach in an area in which he had earlier done research but more recently lost interest. The course in Middle Eastern Politics was reassigned to PITA's archenemy. The rationale was to make optimal use of the department's teaching resources.

A scientific Dr. PITA had received a large grant and had a project going full-steam in her lab, which she claimed was about to produce major results. In connection with long-planned renovations to the building, the chair said her lab would have to be dismantled in preparation for a move. Construction was delayed and plans changed part-way through. After consulting with the insurance company, the chair learned that the promised new location was unacceptable. By the time PITA's lab was functioning again, she was nine months behind.

In the face of a long series of minor hassles and torments, it is not unlikely that Dr. PITA will protest, appeal to higher authority, or perhaps file a formal grievance. For this reason, it is important that you send occasional messages that show respect for PITA's status. Tenure is still sacred in academic culture, and any administrator has a great deal to lose if he or she is perceived to be persecuting a professor or trying to drive a professor out.

On the other hand, you will be surprised at how far you can go in tormenting Dr. PITA if the Stage-One condition is met, namely a shared understanding in the academic unit that PITA does not belong. Most professors know little and care less about administrative matters. They are unlikely to challenge your decisions about PITA, no matter how loudly he complains, and they will accept with little questioning your explanation that you have only the department's (faculty's, university's) best interests in mind, that nobody gets what they want all the time, and that in a condition where resources are scarce and everybody is overworked, tough decisions have to be made.

Dr. PITA, for his part, will feel stress. Having the high opinion of himself typical of professors, and encouraged by some reference group outside his home academic unit, he will be put off-balance by the negative messages you send. He may resist hearing them. He may consult a psychiatrist, worried that he is becoming paranoid. Most of the pitas in my study reported a "sinking feeling," an inability to breathe, or a feeling of some shroud being pulled over them, when they physically entered their workplaces while Stage Two was underway.

Most cases end after the administrative hassling has proceeded for some length of time, typically two to five years. Optimally, Dr. PITA moves to a position elsewhere, takes early retirement, gets sick, or dies.

Regrettably, the last decade of the twentieth century has brought an oversupply of Ph.D.'s on many academic markets, and shrinking numbers of positions available. Dr. PITA may not find it easy to move. Further, given that professors in some fields do much of their work at home or otherwise off-campus, Dr. PITA may be able to insulate herself sufficiently from the negative appraisal of her employer to stay healthy. She may be a "tough old bird." In Stage Three, she officially becomes a "case."

8

Millennial fears

If sterner measures are required for PITA's elimination, a skilled administrator will be acutely sensitive to the temper of the times. If PITA is not gone after years of subtle Stage-Two torment, an explicit, overt move will not likely scare him away. As an administrator, you have to anticipate his appeals not just to higher authority within the university corporation but to outside influences: the discipline or profession he belongs to, the national professors' organization, the courts, and the media. Any formal case against PITA must therefore be constructed in such a way as to take advantage of public opinion and popular culture.

Examples from history illustrate the point. In most of Europe until the end of World War II, hatred of Jews was woven into the social fabric. In this context, a university dean or rector seeking to dislodge Professor PITA from his chair might understandably search for evidence that he was of Jewish ancestry, held seders, avoided pork, or was allied with Jewish causes. Even a hint of Jewish ties could be enough to taint Professor PITA in the popular mind, both on-campus and off, and make his position untenable.

In parts of the United States a century ago, the cultural climate was so firmly Christian that public doubts about Dr. PITA's orthodoxy—his fascination with Darwin's theory of evolution, for example—were enough to make even a thin case against him stick. Especially in the South, Dr. PITA could be brought into disrepute by suggestions that he advocated interracial marriage. The aforementioned W. I. Thomas was fired from Chicago in 1918 on a charge (later dropped) of having registered in a hotel under a false name, but newspapers highlighted his "eccentric" views on sex, in particular that women should enjoy as much sexual freedom as men, and have access to birth control.

In the most celebrated wave of professorial eliminations in recent U.S. history, administrators picked up on the widespread fear of communism in the 1950s. In the climate epitomized by the public hearings of Senator Joseph McCarthy, it was not necessary that Dr. PITA be proven to be a member of an illegal political organization. To ensure his discrediting, it was enough that he be shown to have once been friends with members of groups that were connected to other groups subsequently deemed suspect by the U.S. government.

The terms *hysteria, panic,* and *witchhunt* are often applied to these movements of the past, which formed the cultural context for dismissal of professors from universities. The implication is that it was wrong to associate the Dr. PITA's of the day with whatever was then most feared, as a way of facilitating their elimination.

My purpose is not to debate fine points of ethics, but to provide academic administrators with practical advice based on 25 case-studies from real life, and related historical research. Collective hysteria is nothing more than shared singleminded devotion to an oversimplified ideal. An administrator who wants to rid his or her academic unit of a tenacious destructive presence, but who is unwilling to tap into whatever hysteria is ongoing in the culture at large, is neglecting an available resource.

An additional benefit from harmonizing your local, particular objective with fears and panics in the larger society is to strengthen a sense of unity and team effort in your academic unit. The American journalist Thad Snow, on the basis of his experience with anti-black hysteria in the South, wrote that it "unifies a community or an area more completely than a flood or any other disaster that I know of ... and many people who normally live on the very fringe of a community's affairs find themselves important in a street-corner discussion or at a big indignation meeting, and they feel warm and worshipful toward community leaders whom they may have envied before." Snow's point applies equally to the academic community whose leader you are.

Fear of Jews, blacks, atheists, sexual libertines and communists has by no means disappeared from the culture of English-speaking North America, but none of these currently matches the fear of violent individuals. Surveys document enormous fear of being robbed, shot, raped, murdered or beaten up, even while statistics suggest declines in many forms of violent crime in many locales. The late historian, Christopher Lasch, wrote insightfully about the priority on personal survival in contemporary culture. It may be that this priority has bred a heightened fear of being personally victimized. Rates of violent crime are indeed high, of course, relative to the 1950s and earlier.

Whatever the reason, today's popular culture seethes with anxiety at the prospect of falling prey to serial killers, mass murderers, rapists, home invaders, political terrorists, suicide bombers, street muggers, drive-by slayers, child molesters, or wife assaulters.

An especial object of fear and horror is violence against categories of people whom custom and law earlier allowed to be victimized with impunity: women, children, homosexuals, people with disabilities, and members of visible minorities. The horror is all the greater when sexual predation is involved. That contemporary culture is "hung up" on sex and mesmerized by sexual perversion is as banal an observation as a sociologist can make.

In a book like the present one, where the priority is on practical knowledge, speculation as to the causes of contemporary panics and hysterias would be out of place. The important point is that today's mass media, at once the expression and source of popular culture, are held spellbound by the outwardly normal and upright citizen who is secretly violent, cruel and depraved.

Paul Bernardo is a prototype of the kind of evil most feared in our time. As the 1990s began in the quiet city of St. Catherine's on the shore of Lake Ontario, he and his battered wife Karla Homolka were kidnapping, torturing, raping and murdering young women, and recording it all on video, so as to be able to relive the pleasure over and over. He was the devil in disguise. People in our time are very much on the lookout for other disguises the devil of predation on the weak and powerless may be wearing, and they collectively feast on occasions when that devil is unmasked.

The lesson for you, as an academic manager intent on excelling in your job, is that if your Dr. PITA can somehow be associated with violence or sexual predation, you stand a much better chance of eliminating him from your workplace. You must be careful not to make charges that are completely without foundation. On the other hand, you should not overlook ways to connect Dr. PITA to the principal fears with which our culture is entering the new millennium.

The possibility that you are dealing with a violent person is worth pondering. The hassles to which Dr. PITA has been subjected in Stage Two may bring to the surface tendencies toward violence until now held in check. Has Dr. PITA perhaps gone into a fit of rage in your office, shaking his fist at you? Has she said or done something that could be interpreted as a threat of doing physical harm to others? Is there anything peculiar or erratic about his behaviour, such that some of the women in your academic unit have become afraid of him?

Similarly, you should carefully consider any evidence that he may be a sexual predator. Are there real or attempted sexual relations in his history with someone who might not have given full consent—one of his students, for example, or a staff member subject to his authority? Has he ever kissed, hugged, embraced, brushed against, or touched somebody who was displeased by this physical contact? If he lives alone, is there suspicion about the ways in which he might be obtaining sexual gratification? If he has been married for a long time, might it be because he has kept his wife physically or emotionally under a spell of domination? Does he seem to enjoy the company of children?

Virtually all the administrators in the cases I have reviewed, were attentive to questions like these, and responsive when Dr. PITA's colleagues or students raised them. They are questions you, too, should ask, in light of the case to be reviewed after an update on my own affairs.

9

October 4, 1997

A week passes quickly when you're working. In any line of work, the time of culmination, when at last "it all comes out," is a rush.

The Outside Judge's report did not arrive this week. No surprise. This gift of a pause from the fray is still with me.

We have a pause from autumn, too. Today we ate dinner outside. The sumac and burning bushes are ablaze, and the maples are beginning to turn, but the thermometer reads high summer. This Sabbath day, here at home, surrounded by trees older than Canada and beneath a clear blue sky, in touch and love with people I know by name (I got an e-mail today from my 95-year-old mother in Missouri, and I sent one back), I could feel the largeness of the world. From this feeling this book is born.

This place is so unlike that place on campus where I have felt most closely the constricting squeeze of institutional control. It is Room 3043 of Needles Hall. That is where Ethics Hearing Committee 94-3 held its first meeting on April 15, 1994—the tribunal that found me guilty of "attacking the character and competence" of a female colleague. It is also where Ethics Hearing Committee 96-1 held its first meeting on May 17, 1996—the tribunal that found me guilty of saying something in class that sounded racist to a student.

Room 3043 is small, maybe twenty feet square. It is devoid of colour, so unlike my study or the woods outside. Everything is

off-white or buff or beige. Six tables are pushed together to make
a big one, and there are fifteen or twenty chairs around it. That
is all.

Room 3043 at first seems windowless, but then you see a
small alcove in the far corner with a beige-curtained window in it.
The window does not open. If you crashed through it you would
not be outside, but only in a hallway. Windows on the other side
of the hallway admit sunlight, but they lead nowhere either. If you
crashed through them, you would be in a roofless, walled-in court
on the top floor of Needles Hall. It is where the provost goes to
smoke.

Maybe, when this time has passed, Room 3043 will be
made into a shrine to the freedom of expression essential to a
university. If the library has a first edition of Orwell's *Nineteen
Eighty-Four*, or a medieval manuscript of Plato's *Apology*, it could
be put on display there, along with artifacts from proceedings of
the University of Waterloo Ethics Committee.

The deadlines the Outside Judge has missed remind me
of one I tried to postpone in 1994. After Ethics Committee 94-3
had delivered its finding of my guilt and recommended that I be
required to accept its finding and make a public apology to my
colleague, and after the provost had accepted these
recommendations, and when I wanted to appeal his decision to
the president, but when the grievance committee demanded that
I proceed immediately to its hearing of essentially the same case
the ethics committee had just ruled on—that was when a
colleague and I went personally to the provost and asked him to
extend the grievance committee's deadline until after my appeal
to the president could be heard. He said no, that the most
extension he could give me was twenty-four hours.

How come the Outside Judge, the provost, and the
president get by with exceeding policy deadlines by two months or
three months or six months, for no apparent reason, but I am

given one day's reprieve even when I have a good reason for requesting more?

I was fantasizing this week about sending a letter to all the deans and other senior administrators at the Outside Judge's university, explaining to them how far this fellow has exceeded the deadline specified in his official terms of reference, and asking them please not to bother him until he finishes his report. If you were in my shoes, would you do that? Would you ever be in my shoes? Why or why not? The question is worth one hundred percent of the mark.

10

Which Lesson from Fabrikant?

An academic administrator's worst nightmare came true on August 24, 1992, at Concordia University in Montreal. Something snapped inside Dr. Valery Fabrikant, Associate Professor of Mechanical Engineering. Storming into his workplace with a high-powered rifle, he shot four professors dead and gravely wounded a fifth.

It was not the worst mass murder in Canadian university history. On December 6, 1989, at *l'Ecole Polytechnique* in the same city, an anti-feminist fanatic had killed fourteen women and wounded thirteen more. The Fabrikant slayings merit scrutiny here, however, because they were the culmination of a mismanaged process of eliminating an undesirable professor.

The process was successful in that this quintessential Dr. PITA was indeed eliminated. He was convicted of murder and put in prison, where he remains. But four professors lost their lives in the process, a fifth almost did, and in the aftermath the rector, academic vice-rector, and other administrators lost their jobs.

To salvage lessons from the tragedy, Concordia's Board of Governors commissioned two investigations. Harry Arthurs, former president of York University in Toronto, headed a three-person team to investigate Fabrikant's accusations of corruption in the Engineeering Faculty. John Scott Cowan, former vice-president at Carleton University in Ottawa, was charged with studying Fabrikant's employment history and drawing conclusions for human resource management. Both Arthurs's and Cowan's reports attempt diagnoses of what went wrong.

The case began in December, 1979, when Fabrikant showed up in Montreal. He was by then an accomplished scientist, with a doctorate and research publications from his native Russia. A professor at Concordia hired him immediately as his research assistant.

Fabrikant did good work and moved up quickly in the professor's research unit. By 1983, he held the title of Research Associate Professor. In 1990, he moved from soft money to regular probationary status. By to the collective agreement, he had the right to be considered for tenure during 1991-92.

Over the first decade of his employment, however, Concordia's senior management had identified Fabrikant as Dr. PITA. In 1982, there was a rape charge against him—though the complaint was dropped. In 1983, a run-in between Fabrikant and the instructor of a French course he was taking resulted in his being banned from courses in continuing education. In 1988, Fabrikant went into a rage when a laser printer he had ordered arrived late. Fabrikant was exceedingly aggressive in pursuing his own interests and complained often about being treated unfairly.

By 1990, the academic vice-rector and her associates were well into a Stage-Two campaign to hassle Fabrikant out of his job. He wrote to her that spring, inquiring about his teaching load and sabbatical. She stonewalled, making what Cowan calls a "fuzzy and unhelpful" response. In October 1990, she wrote to Fabrikant that she considered him to be harassing her and her staff, and she threatened discipline. She ignored his right to be considered for tenure. At a Senate meeting late in 1991, the associate vice-rector had Fabrikant searched, for fear he was carrying a gun.

Perhaps the clearest flaw in the process of Fabrikant's elimination is that the vice-rector commenced Stage Two before

Stage One was far enough along. She was systematically trying to get rid of him while the dean, department chair, and other professors in engineering still considered him a worthy—if abrasive—colleague. Fabrikant could thus play the higher level of management off against the lower one. Indeed, in December, 1991, Fabrikant won renewal of his probationary appointment for 1992-93.

By this time, however, Stage Three had commenced: open warfare of the institution upon Dr. PITA. Fabrikant was circulating by e-mail charges of serious misconduct by engineering professors: false claims to authorship of research, diversion of research funds for personal aggrandizement, and conflicts of interest. In two letters to the Board of Governors in February and April, 1992, Fabrikant demanded that his charges be investigated.

Both letters were entrusted to the academic vice-rector, who made no serious investigation but simply reported back that Fabrikant's allegations were unfounded. In June, she and another vice-rector asked the rector to suspend Fabrikant. The rector declined.

Stage Three was formalized. In July, the dean tried to reclaim grant money from Fabrikant and to assign him for the coming year to teach courses outside his interests and expertise. In August, university lawyers sent Fabrikant a registered letter threatening dismissal and court proceedings "to compel you to cease your current plan of action." On August 24, Fabrikant opened fire.

Along with all right-minded observers, Arthurs and Cowan agree that Fabrikant alone was responsible for the murders and that he might have committed his crimes no matter what the administrators had done earlier. Still, implicit in both reports is a lesson about how things might have turned out differently.

Arthurs was placed in an awkward position by his terms of reference, which required his committee to assess the truth or falsity of accusations made by a man already convicted of a heinous crime. To make matters worse, the committee found that many of Fabrikant's accusations were true. He had claimed to have been a "scientific prostitute": paid to provide his superiors with research results on which they then placed their names. This appeared to have been so. Many of the financial irregularities Fabrikant had alleged proved to be essentially correct.

The committee might have chalked up to bizarre coincidence the fact that this murderous Dr. PITA had also noticed academic misconduct by others. Instead, the committee lambasts what it called the "production-driven research culture"—the system currently in place in most universities for achieving excellence, whereby professors are rewarded for grants they bring in and articles they turn out. This culture, the committee claims, tempts people to misappropriate credit for work done, to place themselves in conflicts of interest, and even to commit fraud. The committee seems to doubt the value of entrepreneurship in academic life, and to cling to older conceptions of professorial autonomy and tenure.

While admitting that current university culture is unlikely soon to change, the Arthurs Committee seems to favour a return to "the project of free intellectual inquiry to which it [the academic community] has been historically committed." The practical implication is that administrators should take seriously and investigate charges like those Fabrikant made at Concordia. This noble advice will appeal to administrators who enjoy opening cans of worms.

Most administrators will find Cowan's advice of more immediate practical value. He confronts head-on the traditional sanctity of individual rights in universities, and says collective rights deserve higher priority. He faults Concordia for treating Fabrikant too benignly from the start, and says administrators should not be so reluctant "to exercise management rights."

Cowan laments that ethics tribunals in universities adopt a criminal rather than civil burden of proof, saying this makes "discipline for ethical violations as rare as hen's teeth."

Cowan cites with approval the professor whose research grants paid Fabrikant's salary during his first seven years at Concordia. That professor, says Cowan, had an autocratic management style that succeeded "with not inconsiderable success" in keeping Fabrikant in line. Cowan urges administrators to say to professors, "I am your employer," and to instruct them as to what they should do. Deans, in particular, should behave as line managers and not be so passive as the dean in this case was.

Cowan acknowledges that if Fabrikant had been suspended or dismissed earlier, or barred from campus by a restraining order, he might still have committed mass murder. The risk of violent revenge by an eliminated professor, however low, can never be ruled out. Academic managers who adopt the harder managerial line Cowan advises may also wish to tighten campus security.

Stage Three: the Incident

The blacklist was a time of evil and ... no one on either side who survived it came through untouched by evil. Caught in a situation that had passed beyond the control of mere individuals, each person reacted as his nature, his needs, his convictions, and his particular circumstances compelled him to. There was bad faith and good, honesty and dishonesty, courage and cowardice, selflessness and opportunism, wisdom and stupidity, good and bad on both sides; and almost every individual involved, no matter where he stood, combined some or all of these antithetical qualities in his own person, in his own acts.

Novelist and screenwriter Dalton Trumbo, in *Additional Dialogue*, 1970; along with others of the "Hollywood Ten," Trumbo had defied the House Un-American Activities Committee in 1947, and been imprisoned for contempt.

11

Deep trouble

The initial stages of Dr. PITA's elimination are subtle, involving (Stage One) informal ostracization from the professorial community and (Stage Two) administrative put-downs and hassles under the guise of routine decision-making. Stage Three normally commences with a particular incident that "brings things out into the open."

By the word *incident* I mean an occurrence or event that, in so far as it becomes public knowledge, confirms that Dr. PITA does not belong in the university. The relevant administrators may not actually make it public, in the sense of announcing it in a memorandum, the campus newspaper, or the public press. As a real or pretended favour to Dr. PITA, or under a requirement of university policy, they may keep the incident secret initially or indefinitely. What is crucial is that they share an understanding that whatever has happened makes Dr. PITA unfit to continue in his position as before, and that they have communicated this to him. The incident places him in "deep trouble" with his employer, and he knows it. It is the kind of event that is subject to oblique comment in campus gossip: "I'm told there was an incident three weeks ago, I don't know the details, but I know it is being taken quite seriously..."

The grapevine also has it that the incident "has been discussed at the highest levels of the university." This may or may not be true, but Stage Three necessarily involves the middle, decanal level of the administrative hierarchy, if not senior management. In a large university, the first two stages may have gone on for years inside Dr. PITA's department, without the president and vice-president even knowing who she is. The incident is a common way they find out, as the chair fills them in on this "longstanding problem" and insists that "now, at last, something has to be done." In other cases, Dr. PITA is already well known to the higher-level administrators, one of whom may be leading the process of eliminating her.

The incident consists of some action on Dr. PITA's part that can be construed as a grievous breach of academic norms. The relevant administrator has to describe the incident with utmost care, so as to appeal to whichever norms are currently paramount in academic and public culture. I know of no recent case of a professor being eliminated for teaching Marxism, espousing racial integration, or tolerating premarital sex.

In our time, the most likely violations cited in administrators' descriptions of the incident are as follows:

- Sexual harassment or abuse: words or actions with an intended or attributed sexual connotation, deemed objectionable by one or more women.
- Racial harassment or abuse: words or actions considered prejudicial or hateful by one or more members of a visible minority, often people of black slave ancestry.
- Threats of violence: words or actions taken to indicate an intention to do physical harm to another.
- Financial wrongdoing: diversion of research funds or other money under university control for personal gain or some other illegitimate purpose.
- Research fraud, including plagiarism: willful misrepresentation of the truth in scholarly writing.
- Absence from campus, consulting, or employment elsewhere

without prior authorization.
- Neglect of key job requirements like submitting students' final grades or completing a specifically assigned task.

The incident allows the administrator to say to Dr. PITA, sometimes in so many words, "Gotcha!" or "Now I'm going to nail you." The grounds cited are often multiple. In an incident where Dr. PITA had taken a group of students on a field trip, he was deemed guilty of mishandling funds *and* putting the students' safety at risk *and* sexual assault. In another case, Dr. PITA was pronounced guilty of sexually harassing a lab assistant *and* making racist jokes. Sometimes the additive principle is applied in a different way. No single statement or action on Dr. PITA's part is identified as constituting sexual harassment, but a succession of seemingly innocuous statements—comments during lectures, for instance—collectively constitute a sexual-harassment incident that cannot be ignored.

One normative breach that is commonly added to other charges is uncollegiality. Showing respect for fellow practitioners of the same discipline or profession has long, of course, been essential to academic life. At a time of unprecedented "tightening up" and emphasis on teamwork, collegiality has become an even higher value. In the present context, disagreement with work-mates over theoretical or administrative issues can itself be seen as a violation of collegiality and legitimate cause for disciplinary action, the more so when this is on top of another offense. To show that Dr. PITA's colleagues are solidly committed to some currently paramount value like gender equality, racial equality, financial propriety, or research ethics, while he has broken ranks, is an effective way to present the case.

Whatever the specific charges, their source is clear to the academic manager who makes them: Dr. PITA's selfish nature, his unwillingness or inability to take other people's interests and feelings into account. Bear in mind the objective here, defined in a classic article entitled "The Conditions of Successful Degradation Ceremonies" as "the ritual destruction of the person denounced." To allow that Dr. PITA's transgressions may be due to an innocent misunderstanding on his part is no way to get rid of him. The claim instead is that he is so wrapped up in himself, and in the gratification of his own needs, that he cruelly tramples on the rights of others and thereby undermines the welfare of the group. The portrayal of Dr. PITA as fundamentally anti-social, callous and insensitive to others' needs, is essential to the later stages of his elimination.

Sexual harassment allegations are especially useful. Dr. PITA is portrayed as hungering for his private sexual satisfaction, and intruding for this purpose on selfless lovers of humanity. Similarly, if Dr. PITA is accused of dishonest disboursements from his research grant, and if his defense that this was to assist a penurious student is acknowledged, the case against him is weak. The real reason for his misconduct needs to be shown to be his personal greed for filthy lucre. Dr. PITA has personality problems. He is impossible to work with. No one can get along with him.

Metaphysical terms like *good* and *evil* have mostly been ruled out of academic discourse in this postmodern era. Administrators are well-advised to avoid them. Still, the incident that begins the third stage in the elimination process means for practical purposes that the academic community (department, faculty, university) has risen up to assert its moral superiority over a miscreant. Jehovah has taken on the Wicked One. But the story is not over. A true Dr. PITA adopts Satan's attitude, as Milton reported it:

What though the field be lost?
All is not lost; th'unconquerable will,
And study of revenge, immortal hate,
And courage never to submit or yield.

12

Sanctions

In the handling of the incident that precipitates Stage Three, an administrator usually emerges as Chief Eliminator. This role may have been vacant until now. Dr. PITA may have been accumulating enemies across campus and widening his reputation as a maker of mischief, but with no one identified as leader of a movement to expel him. As the process becomes formal, somebody assumes this responsibility. In the case of Dr. Fabrikant at Concordia, it was the academic vice-rector. More often it is the faculty dean. More rarely, it is a department or committee chair.

Upon the chief eliminator falls the duty not only to set down in writing the nature of the incident, what it involved and why it is intolerable, but to define the appropriate punishment. The chief eliminator does not accuse. Ideally, accusations have been made by one or more other people—about which more later. The chief eliminator's task is to pronounce Dr. PITA guilty of the accusations and impose sanctions. There is probably not a presumption of innocence, nor what is usually understood by the term "fair trial." The administrator makes discreet consultations and some kind of investigation, probably calls PITA on the carpet "to discuss the matter," and then makes a determination on behalf of the collective as to what should be done. The chief eliminator behaves as the symbolic embodiment of the academic unit, of the values it celebrates and the purposes it serves.

The result is a letter whose salutation, even if first names have been used until then, is probably "Dear Dr. PITA." The letter may be sent quickly, to catch PITA off guard, hit her hard and fast, and urge a speedy exit. More likely, weeks pass as the chief eliminator consults with senior management, the university's lawyers, the police, psychiatrists, rank-and-file professors, students, or whoever else. Delay has the advantage of allowing the case to be made more carefully, and of keeping PITA in a limbo of unease. On the other hand, delay allows PITA time to anticipate sanctions and prepare her defense.

The administratively cleanest content of the letter is outright dismissal. But this so-called "capital punishment of labour relations" assumes what most university policies call "adequate cause." The misconduct has to be (the language of Waterloo's policy is fairly standard) "of such a serious nature as to render the faculty member clearly unfit to hold a tenured appointment."

In many cases, the chief eliminator is unwilling to risk a decision to dismiss, for fear that in a culture where tenure is still sacred, the case will be deemed too weak and the dismissal overturned on appeal by the president, an arbitrator, or whatever higher authority is provided for in university policy. Outright dismissal may mean going farther out on a limb than prudence allows. The administrator could in the end be left there very much alone.

The more likely content of the chief eliminator's letter is a set of punishments that stop short of dismissal, but that humiliate Dr. PITA sufficiently that she will leave through some other exit-door. Until the last couple of centuries, the word *humiliate* usually referred to the physical act of bowing or prostration, as a gesture for acknowledging the worthlessness of an individual in the face of a worthy personage. Since that time, the word is more often used metaphorically, to refer to a procedure that lowers somebody's dignity or self-respect in the face of an established, respectable group. Hawthorne's *Scarlet Letter* is the literary archetype.

In a thoughtful recent book entitled *Humiliation*, William Ian Miller distinguishes this bruising technique of exclusion from shame. The latter, he writes, "operates by stripping someone of a status she had some right to before the particular failing, whereas humiliation destroys the illusion of having belonged at all." Dr. PITA is beyond shame. She is *shameless*. In previous years the group has sent her hundreds of teasing, cajoling messages, subtle cues that she was behaving outside its boundaries and thereby losing a respectable status within it. She just didn't get it. She didn't shape up. Now the group has the goods on her. The incident allows the group to bring its full weight down. Humiliation, says Miller, is rough justice.

The findings of an *ad hoc* committee appointed to deal with an unusually tenacious Dr. PITA illustrate the kind of statements an official letter of humiliation may include. The first two stages of his elimination were already far advanced, to the point that the president and vice-president were expressing fear that Dr. PITA was going to do them physical violence. A three-person committee was at this point established to investigate and make recommendations.

As is customary, the committee affirmed PITA's "academic and scholarly gifts, his contributions to the institution, and our desire that a way be found to work out these difficulties so that he can become a more productive and effective member of the faculty." Immediately thereafter, however, the committee gave him its "firm and unequivocal counsel that the patterns of destructive behaviour to which he is prone in relationships with administration and colleagues must be radically altered. We believe that his prospects of staying depend upon his restructuring his way of dealing with his dissatisfactions and disagreements."

The committee then made six recommendations. First was that he seek professional counselling, at the institution's expense, toward the end of eliminating his verbal abuse and threats, "and the development of cooperative negotiation skills."

Second, he "must apologize sincerely and unconditionally" to the vice-president and president, for his verbally aggressive and abusive pattern of behaviour.

Third, he "must refrain from discussing his grievances with persons outside the institution, or even inside the institution, unless he has tried all collegial means to process the grievances in a collegial way with the persons directly involved."

Fourth, he "must exhibit a willingness to reach agreements with the administration and to stick with them."

Fifth, he "must exhibit a willingness to accept the needs and interests of the college in the definition of his job description and in the setting of his teaching/research load."

Sixth, he "must develop a reasonable tolerance for the normal kinds of insensitivities and mistakes made by normal people, including especially those of his superiors."

The committee went on to say that if Dr. PITA "is unwilling to accept the conditions we have identified as essential to his positive functioning," he should seek a position at some other institution. The committee recommended that he be offered a contractually limited, one-year appointment, with the possibility of return to the tenure stream if he could demonstrate "substantial progress in solving the problems we have identified."

The committee also said the president and vice-president should apologize to Dr. PITA "for the introduction into hearings of the hearsay from others alleging his potential for physical violence." It said the president should also apologize for "the provocative act" of sending him ads for positions elsewhere.

The unvarnished quality of the written findings against Dr. PITA in this case makes them especially useful as illustration. This group's claim to supremacy over the individual is blunt. The dissenter is forbidden even to discuss his dissent outside the group and he is explicitly told to tolerate his superiors' mistakes. Dr. PITA's problem is as Milton said, "th'unconquerable will." The only solution is "exhibit a willingness." Yet this definition itself precludes a solution. Dr. PITA could not acquiesce to these recommendations, "humble himself" so to speak, without admitting that he had already "blown his chance." Submission to his institution's expectations under duress would demonstrate that he does not belong there anyway, since he was officially found to have failed to submit freely.

A once popular song said there must be fifty ways to leave your lover. There are at least as many different ways a university can abandon a professor, as witness the diverse kinds of penalty letter that are alike in crushing or humiliating Dr. PITA enough that he is no longer able to "hold his head up." The letter's effect, if not its avowed purpose, is to take Dr. PITA off the moral payroll, to deprive him of the sense of self-worth required to walk across campus, stand in front of a class, and teach. This may not end the case, of course. Dr. PITA may put up a fight, as he did in the case above for three and a half more years. Normally, however, the period after the incident and letter of penalty is one of progressive withering on the vine. It is only a matter of time before the professor leaves—whether through early retirement, long-term disability, suicide, or however else.

Administrators should never underestimate the moral power they hold over professors in their employ. It is more of a weapon than most realize. An Associate Dean who seized upon a student complaint against a professor of exceptional renown, turning it into "the incident" that led to the man's departure, was able to reduce that proud, accomplished pita to words of utter abandonment, just by setting down a written account of the incident and declaring that it would be kept on file:

I want more than anything to be a good person, a humane, strong and caring person. I love so much teaching and studying. I want so much to be able to do these things and to be loved. To the extent that I am able to rationalize I see myself as good, but my colleagues seem to know that I'm not worth much at all. I'm scared silly. I'm scared of my sons seeing me a despised old man. I have no future without this university. I gave it my best try years ago. I'm really afraid that I don't meet the requirements but it's too late to drop the course. Collect my bad marks if you must.

13

The small matter of truth

No sarcasm is intended in the title above. Truth is a large matter to philosophers. It is what universities are for. Waterloo's motto is *Concordia cum veritate,* "In harmony with truth."

But our purpose here is practical, not philosophic or inspirational. The point of these few pages is that in the process of eliminating Dr. PITA, administrators need to be mildly, but only mildly, concerned with truth. An insightful new book is subtitled *The Assault on Truth in American Law.* Academic managers with time to spare should read it. Others can be content with the implications offered here.

The issue will arise. Dr. PITA will claim that the charges against him are exaggerated, trumped up, or otherwise false. "The truth," he will plead, "is that out of hostility to me and in an effort to destroy my reputation and career, certain parties have used slander to fabricate a case against me. I am innocent and I will not rest until my name is cleared." If the case against him has been crafted with care, PITA's pleadings will sound hollow as a pipe.

Arbitrators, tribunals, and the public use not one but a variety of yardsticks to assess the truth of accusations of wrongdoing. Here are seven different ones:

- **Victim's views.** Do one or more sincere victims of the alleged wrongdoing support the accusations?

- **Witnesses' views.** Do they corroborate the accusations?
- **PITA's record.** Are other of his actions consistent with what he is accused of now?
- **Character witnesses for the accuser.** Do they vouch for the accuser's honesty and integrity?
- **Official finding.** Has a responsible person or committee already made a finding of Dr. PITA's guilt?
- **Dr. PITA's admissions.** Do they support the accusations?
- **Hard evidence.** Does physical evidence support the accusations?

For deciding whether an accusation is true or false, people who watch crime dramas on TV normally think of the last yardstick on the list. A dead body, bruises and broken bones, fingerprints on a gun, blood-stained clothing, written records showing who did what when, where stolen property was found, results of DNA testing—this is the kind of hard evidence on which the truth of the charges and the fate of the accused are imagined to depend. If the case against the accused is based only on circumstantial or hearsay evidence, or if it comes down to one person's word against another's, the accused probably goes free. Innocence is assumed unless guilt is proven beyond reasonable doubt.

Real-life criminal cases do sometimes proceed in this way. The point here is that the case against Dr. PITA, if it is to be won, must proceed in a different way. The hard-evidence yardstick must be kept out of consideration. So must the presumption of innocence and the requirement of proof beyond reasonable doubt.

If you, as an administrator, are willing to wait until PITA leaves dead bodies in the hallway, as Fabrikant did at Concordia, or provides you with similar conclusive evidence of his deservedness of elimination, you do not need this book. You are reading it because you do not want to wait. You want him gone sooner rather than later. You therefore distract the relevant authorities, including public opinion, from questions of hard evidence, and give them other yardsticks for deciding whether the charges against PITA are true or false. Five practical principles serve this end.

First, formulate the indictment against PITA in such a way that hard evidence does not apply. The primordial case of elimination of an undesirable teacher can serve as a model. Socrates was accused of misleading and corrupting youth, of making the worse appear the better cause, and of believing either in the wrong gods or none at all. The truth of these charges did not turn on physical evidence. DNA testing would not have helped, even had it been available. The prosecution won its case.

In the current cultural context, the charges most likely to stick are similarly "squishy" or intangible. All of the following are drawn from cases in my study:

bullying	leering
making threats	corrupting procedures
abuse	incivility
arousing fear in others	uncollegiality
unauthorized conduct	failure to disclose
breach of confidentiality	misrepresentation
bad academic citizenship	breach of trust
interference in others' work	intimidation
equivocation	confrontation
attacking integrity	conflict of interest.

A special strength of many such accusations is elasticity, their applicability in common parlance to a range of behaviour stretching from good turns to foibles to crimes.

The second principle is to highlight the yardsticks at the beginning of the list. Coddle and reward anyone who claims to have been victimized by Dr. PITA, especially if the victim is young, female, aboriginal, nonwhite, disabled, a single parent, or in another category of legally designated or generally recognized oppressed people. Encourage the victim to make a written statement of her belief that the accusations against Dr. PITA are true. Search out others who will corroborate her story as character witnesses or even better, as witnesses to her emotional distress at the time of the incident and afterwards.

With adroit application of this principle, a situation will be defined wherein one or more innocent victims, supported by upright witnesses whose only interest is the common good, stand on one side declaring Dr. PITA's guilt, while on the other side PITA stands alone. No authority or observer can then find the accusations against him to be false, without calling into question the honesty and integrity of those whose lives he has damaged.

The third principle is to emphasize the institutional yardstick, an official finding of PITA's guilt. For most of history, this by itself has been enough. Harvey Cox began his examination of the Vatican's silencing of liberation theologian Leonardo Boff by quoting the classic Latin proverb: "Once Rome has spoken, the case is closed." In the Catholic as in some other churches, ecclesiastical authority defines the difference between truth and error—and error has no rights.

Your institution lacks the strength of Rome. Yet once an administrator acting as chief eliminator sets down in writing a description of the incident, a finding of PITA's guilt, and a call for sanctions, that statement carries weight. It undermines the presumption of innocence and provides all who subsequently judge the charges with a yardstick that shows them to be true.

If the first stage of PITA's elimination has been carried out, she is already known as an "enemy of the people." If the second stage has proceeded apace and petty torments have been applied, she should be showing signs of stress and acting strange. If news now comes of an incident involving misconduct so serious as to warrant formal recognition and punishment by the authorities, it will be seen to confirm earlier impressions and be taken as the truth. "I always knew there was something funny about her," people will say in hushed tones.

The fourth principle is to make use, if possible, of the yardstick of Dr. PITA's own admissions. A full confession is unlikely. Pitas undoubtedly exist who admit guilt and beg for mercy, but no cases in my research are of this kind.

Yet curiously, nearly all the pitas in my study went a long way voluntarily toward corroborating the accusations, as if trying to help out their accusers as much as possible. "I did kiss her, but with no sexual intent." "In my anger I did threaten to punish those who have done me wrong, but I did not mean this in the sense of physical harm." "I did use the word *vagina* in the conversation, but I did not mean it as a put-down of women." The undesirable professors in my study seem to have a keen sense of empirical truth, so much that they help dig their own graves. It is easy for an administrator to spotlight how much of the allegations Dr. PITA has admitted to, leaving to hearers' imaginations how much worse was what actually happened.

Fifth and finally, as J. S. Cowan urged in his report on Concordia, a civil as opposed to criminal standard of proof must be insisted on. The chief eliminator should not be expected to prove Dr. PITA's guilt beyond reasonable doubt. That the balance of probabilities goes against him should be enough. His life is not at stake, only his job in this one workplace. If, as measured by the first six yardsticks on the list, the evidence inclines toward the truth of the accusations, they should be accepted. In the cases at my university, to the extent that anybody knew the difference between civil and criminal burdens of proof, the former was considered to suffice.

If the five principles given above are followed, admnistrators need not concern themselves further with the actual, empirical truth of the charges against Dr. PITA. The point is to keep hard, physical evidence off the table and out of play. A case where graphic physical evidence spoiled the show can serve for final emphasis.

A swim coach at a major university was charged with sexual harassment and abuse of a young female swimmer. The university followed the five principles, even though the coach was not in ill repute beforehand. The charges were formulated in squishy language. The victim was coddled. An ethics tribunal brought in a finding of guilt and recommended the coach be fired. He admitted he knew the young woman and that the prospect of a sexual relationship between them had arisen. A civil burden of proof was applied. The university president upheld the tribunal's finding and fired the coach in the spring of 1997.

The university's bad luck was that the coach then went public with hard, physical evidence: e-mails the victim had sent him after the alleged date-rape, offering him sexual favours in unambiguous terms, and including photographs of herself in suggestive poses. It was she who sexually harassed him, the coach claimed. Newspapers leapt at the story. *Macleans* printed one of the pictures. The university's case collapsed. The coach was reinstated. The president went on an extended leave, diagnosed with clinical depression and pilloried in the press.

This case highlights the need for administrative attention to what tangible evidence might show to be the truth. Yet what were the odds of such e-mails and pictures being sent and then being publicly released? Without them, truth would have remained as small a matter as in Socrates's case or most others in my research.

14

October 11, 1997

Today is the feast of St. Kenneth in the Catholic calendar. If I were in Austria, where I taught as a visiting professor before my troubles here began, my name day would be something to celebrate. Here I have remembered it only now, after the sun has set. The day was a celebration anyway. Balmy weather has held all week. At the farmers' market this morning, we strolled in the sun amidst untold thousands of apples, cabbages, beets, chrysanthemums, and out-of-towners here for Oktoberfest.

No word from the Outside Judge again this week. Tiredness of waiting got the best of me on Monday and Tuesday. That and meetings slowed my writing down. I drafted a further fax to the man in whose hands too much of my fate rests:

I appreciated your fax of 25 September, and I do not want to seem insensitive to the "administrative woes" that burden you in your home university. Some of them have been making the news even here.

Still, you will understand how frustrating it is to have been led to expect your report for this university by four successive dates (1 August, 28 August, 10 September, and 3 October), all of which have passed. Could you please provide the provost and me with a further update on the status of the report?

I did not send the fax. At the Outside Judge's university this week, both the graduate students and the staff voted to certify as unions under the Labour Relations Act, and the faculty are expected to do so shortly. The Outside Judge may be worried about hanging onto his own job. I had best leave him be for now.

I worry. In the later stages of elimination processes, an admninistrator's referral of the matter to prominent outsiders is a common and often effective manoeuvre.

One famous example is from outside academia. Two immigrant Italian anarchists, Nicola Sacco and Bartolomeo Vanzetti, were convicted of murder in Massachusetts in 1921. They claimed they were innocent. Hard evidence was on their side. Eyewitnesses placed them somewhere else than the scene of the crime, and another man confessed to it. Even as the two men's appeals were turned down, questions kept being raised about whether they deserved to die. As a last resort, there was an appeal for clemency to the state governor.

On June 1, 1927, the governor appointed a three-man committee to advise him. There was the president of Harvard University, the president of the Massachusetts Institute of Technology, and a judge. The committee's report, released on August 7, found against Sacco and Vanzetti, and they were executed on August 23.

An academic example of the same manoeuvre occurred in 1993. For three years the president of a small institution had nudged Dr. PITA in numerous ways toward the exit-door, but the latter would not budge. The president had then initiated a Strategic Planning Process in which the institution's finances were reviewed and a crisis identified. Insolvency could be avoided only by the elimination of one faculty position, namely Dr. PITA's. His supporters raised pointed questions about whether the crisis was real.

On October 5, 1993, the president appointed a two-person team of consultants to advise him on the institution's financial future. One was a retired university president, the other a retired dean. The consultants presented their report on November 10, 1993, which the president and board of directors took to confirm the threat of unmanageable deficits. On February 28, 1994, the president informed Dr. PITA that as of the end of the current academic year, the institution would no longer require his services.

In a given time and place, people in positions of high responsibility (or recently retired from them) tend to have a common outlook. Their highest priority is usually on preserving the legitimacy of existing institutions. It is hard for any such official, being personally embedded in the established order, to contradict a decision already officially reached. To do so might threaten the stability of the system as a whole.

In my case, the local university president has removed himself altogether from the decision of whether the punishments imposed on me shall stand. The Outside Judge is neither advisor nor consultant. He is acting on the president's behalf. The latter has agreed to accept whatever decision his delegate makes.

The Outside Judge told me he had never met Waterloo's president nor spoken with him on the telephone. He further volunteered that he did not plan to consult with the president in the course of handling my appeal.

Still, the Outside Judge holds a position of high responsibility in the same Ontario university system as the president and provost of Waterloo hold their positions in. How easily could he contradict official decisions already made by his administrative colleagues? Will he risk threatening the stability of a sister institution when unions are threatening the stability of his own?

15

Leading Leymann's mob

Dr. PITA's elimination is the academic expression of a more general social process that has been identified and subjected to careful research. Heinz Leymann, a German psychologist working at the University of Stockholm, Sweden, applied the name *workplace mobbing* to this process in 1984. In a 1990 article in the journal *Victims and Violence*, he provided an English-language summary of his findings. By 1997, he had gathered together the results of his and others' investigations, along with an extensive bibliography and FAQ section, and made all this available in a web-site at http://www.leymann.se/English.

At first glance, Leymann's analysis may appear to be so wrongheaded as to merit scorn. The word *mobbing* implies lawlessness, action without thought, the extreme opposite of the rationality with which you approach academic administration. You cannot contemplate yourself being part of a mob. Nor are you willing to think of Dr. PITA as a victim. It is he who is victimizing the entire academic unit that has him on its faculty. His oddball contrariness, if not outright iniquity, causes the diversion of enormous amounts of time and energy away from the agreed-upon mission of the department, faculty, and university. You cannot stomach a theory that seems to be on Dr. PITA's side.

You should rather keep cool and learn from your enemy. Leymann is indeed on PITA's side. His research (in marked contrast to J. S. Cowan's report on Concordia) is unashamedly rooted in a priority on individual rights. Perhaps reflecting his own circumstance as a German *emigré* teaching in Scandinavia, whose command of Swedish is probably imperfect and strangely accented, Leymann favours high tolerance in workplaces for personal differences and idiosyncracies. He shows weak appreciation of the need for moral solidarity among those who work together, and no appreciation at all for how effective the collective humiliation of a misfit can be for building team spirit and enhancing productivity.

Leymann's biases were pointedly driven home to me not by an academic manager, as you might expect, but by a leftist professor allied with organized labour. Having heard my sketch of Leymann's work in a colloquium, the Marxist professor defended workplace mobbing in cases where a worker breaks ranks with co-workers and tries to curry favour with management. "What else are you going to do with ratebusters, snitches, and scabs?" he asked. "In the war of the workplace, if workers cannot enforce discipline among themselves, for the sake of worker control, they are left at the mercy of the discipline management tries to impose on them for its own purposes."

The leftist professor's comments bring home the essential point: if a workplace is to integrate itself successfully into the globalized economic order of our time, it cannot afford to keep on the payroll an individual who violates group norms and insists on going his or her own way. Whether from the union or management point of view, there is simply no room for the person who marches to the sound of a different drummer. What looks like mobbing to Leymann is merely the unleashing of collective sentiment for the rational purpose of safeguarding and promoting group interests—however these are defined.

Leymann admits on his web-site that his biases have been uncovered even in Sweden. Under the mantle of occupational health and safety, he set up a specialized clinic there in the late 1980s, for "victims" of workplace mobbing. He counselled well over a thousand such people, and his work was publicized across Europe. His interviews with these "victims" brought to light, however, illegal and criminal activities to which they had been subjected, mainly by their employers. Leymann reports that his clinic was therefore boycotted by the Swedish national health-care system, and has since been closed.

Nonetheless, once Leymann's slant toward individual liberty under the law is recognized and corrected, his research findings can be seized upon by academic administrators and applied in a practical way to the solution of real problems in today's university. I have freely drawn upon Leymann's insights throughout this book, and highlight here ten of his most important findings.

- The mobbing process has four phases, similar to the five stages of professorial elimination I offer in this book. Leymann begins with a triggering incident, something that dramatizes the target's separation from the group. Then comes stigmatization through hostile communications toward and about him, messages that hold him up to ridicule. Third is management's acceptance of the prejudices of the target's workmates and the initiation of formal action. The fourth stage is expulsion.

- Mobbing is distinct from the dynamics of normal interaction, wherein each group member's fortunes rise and fall over time. Aided by an instrument called the "Leymann Inventory of Psychological Terrorization," he found mobbing to be an all-or-nothing process that seldom occurs in half-measure.

- The process may be mutual at first, with two workers "going at" each other, but then one of them becomes the underdog and is subjected to collective ostracization.

- The overt reasons for the mobbing often obscure what Leymann calls the "real" reasons, which may be that the worker of concern has a higher skill level or rate of pay than average, or that he or she is a "whistle-blower," outraged at some illegal or unethical practice and determined to put a stop to it.

- The mobbing phenomenon is not uncommon. One survey showed that about one percent of the working population in Norway had at some time been mobbed.
- Mobbing entails sizable costs to the organization. Sometimes a person is paid for years, without being assigned any real work to do. There may be long periods of sick leave, lowered rates of production, and a heavy drain on the time of managers, health professionals, and external consultants.
- The most noticeable consequences for workers who are mobbed are a variety of emotional and psychosomatic disorders. These workers are subjected to what Leymann calls an "overkill" of "ignominious psychiatric examinations and diagnoses." On account of isolation from the work-group, their coping resources tend to break down. They feel helplessness and despair, and rage at their inability to obtain legal redress.
- Because a prospective employer commonly telephones the previous employer for a reference before hiring a job applicant, mobbed workers are often unable to find work at all after expulsion.
- Psychiatrists frequently interpret the mobbed worker's state of mind as a sign of paranoia. Leymann observed a number of cases where the mobbed worker was forcibly detained in a psychiatric hospital for this reason.
- Among possible outcomes of workplace mobbing, suicide ranks high. Between 10 and 15 percent of Swedish suicides have a background of being mobbed at work.

Leymann's sympathies for the target of mobbing lead him to suggest "ameliorative interventions" for preventing the target's expulsion: conciliation by an outside higher authority, access to publicity, an impartial hearing with formal procedures, and so on. Such proposals, rooted as they are in a preoccupation with individual rights, are unlikely to hold much interest for an academic manager faced with a real, live Dr. PITA. They are like proposals of long, tedious, costly, and uncertain medical procedures in the case of a seriously ill or injured patient, when the collective welfare might be better served by quick and painless expiry. Leymann reports himself puzzled to have found not a single case of mobbing where the employer admitted fault and provided the target with redress.

Leymann's puzzlement would be less if he understood and accepted the trend toward corporatism, as John Ralston Saul has described it in *The Unconscious Civilization* and other books. Increasingly, says Saul, legitimacy lies with the group, not the citizen. In Saul's view, we are making a great leap backwards into

the unconscious state beloved of the subject who, existing as a function in any one of the tens of thousands of corporations—public and private—is relieved of personal, distinterested responsiblity for his society....

You may or may not agree with Saul that the leap is backwards, but you know it is real. Will you be dust in the wind or dust underfoot? This book assumes the former: your determination to strengthen the group you lead and to avail yourself of practical knowledge toward this end, even if (like Leymann's) it rests on assumptions you reject.

16

Necessary harm

In the spring of 1994, in the midst of the murder of about a million people in Rwanda, BBC correspondent Fergal Keane made his way into the country and sought out the vice-rector of the University of Butare for an interview. The vice-rector was on the side of the genocidal Hutu militias that were systematically hacking Tutsis to death. Keane asked the administrator if the Tutsis deserved to die.

"Killing is a terrible thing," the vice-rector answered, "but in war people are killed. That is how it happens."

In that same spring of 1994, worlds apart from Rwanda, I learned a woman's story that promotes similar fatalism with respect to workplace mobbing. In large organizations squeezed by the demands of global competition, undesirable workers get eliminated. The harm done is as necessary as killing is in war.

A former student of mine—we had not been in touch for years—telephoned me in a desperate tone and asked if I would meet with him and his wife. She was being sexually harassed at work, he said, and could not get the harassment stopped. They were at wit's end.

I agreed to talk with them. This was just after I had been found guilty of harassing and abusing a female professor and of contributing to a chilly climate for women, and after restrictions on my teaching had been imposed on that account. I was still free, however, to meet with students or former students in distress, and was therefore glad to sit down with the caller and his wife, Ms. PITA.

She was an immigrant to this part of the world. Her accent gave her away. Like her husband, she was shy and soft-spoken. I could tell on first meeting that she was the kind of person who blushes easily. She recounted her story with obvious pain. These are the facts she gave me first.

Her troubles had begun seven years before on the production line of the large factory where she had already worked for many years. She was assigned to a job that paired her with an harassing male. On the basis of her description, I call him here simply the Jerk.

Almost from the start, the Jerk berated Ms. PITA's job performance, belittling her at every opportunity and making repeated comments that she was not up to par. His demeaning chatter gradually became more personal: telling her her teeth were crooked and her clothes were "fucking cheap." By 1989, the harassment had progressed to sexual put-downs: musing out loud about her sex-life and underwear, and making disparaging remarks about her breasts and body.

Once, when Ms. PITA told the Jerk she was going to report him to their boss, he grabbed her by the arm so tightly that it left a bruise. She therefore did complain to the boss, and in the ensuing years, to the boss's boss, to the union, and to the plant management.

In 1992, Ms. PITA began keeping a journal about the Jerk's harassment, her complaints, and the company's inaction. The helplessness, desperation, and rage that Leymann writes about were apparent in every entry. She wrote once that she had asked the Jerk what she had ever done to make him hurt and hate her so much. As time went on, she began to feign illness in order to leave work early or not come in.

Two incidents brought things to a head. In the first, the boss called a meeting for rearranging jobs, and proposed changes that were greatly to PITA's disadvantage. Anger rose in her, and she hit the desk with her fist—a gesture Leymann says is not uncommon at a critical point of the elimination process. Enabled by her anger to use the language of her workmates, PITA told her boss that if he didn't start running his fucking department without the Jerk's help, he was going to lose his own fucking job.

Nine months later, there came a day when PITA fell apart. She began sobbing uncontrollably and was taken to the nurse. Management sent her home, her husband took her to a doctor, and she went on sick leave for several months. It was after her return to work and the same harassment from the Jerk as before that her husband phoned me. By that time, her complaints had reached the head offices of both the company and the union. Meetings, hearings and investigations had taken place, but nothing had changed.

PITA's manner in our meeting had the flat, disengaged quality often observed in post-traumatic stress. Life itself seemed to have been drained out of her. Hysteria over sexual harassment was raging. Newspapers exposed abusers with gleeful regularity. PITA's company had a written policy of zero tolerance. Her union was known for championing women's rights. Its national leader was a paragon of political correctness. Why had nothing been done? PITA was at the end of her rope. So was her husband.

Only as more details of her story emerged did the reality of her situation come into focus. Sexual harassment was only part of it, and a small part at that. The Jerk did not appear really to want sexual favours from PITA. Getting her goat was satisfaction enough for him, an objective achieved by vulgarities and sexually degrading slurs.

PITA had a partial physical disability, the result of an injury long before she was assigned to work with the Jerk. The disability, and the way it was handled under terms of the collective agreement, set PITA apart from her workmates in crucial ways. She was paid at an hourly rate; almost everybody else was on piecework. While other workers rotated among numerous jobs in the unit, PITA was restricted to those not requiring the physical dexterity she had lost in her accident. In addition, PITA had more seniority than most of her workmates, and thus earned more than they for the same amount of work.

Informal differences reinforced these written ones in arousing collective resentment toward PITA in her work group. There was her accent, and her belonging to an ethnic minority distinct from those to which other workers belonged. More important, she was in a moral, even prudish, minority of one. Her workmates, both male and female, took crude banter in stride. They seemed all to have been around the block a few times. PITA had not. She was devoted to her church and her family. Sex for her was a private matter.

The Jerk, too, held an unusual position in the circle of workmates—except that his gave him special power. There was about him a racy bravado, the scent of being on the far side of law, that some female workers found sexy. Further, he had connections for getting things cheap and tax-free. Sometimes, at the end of a shift, the trunk of his car was like a mobile canteen for tobacco and alcohol. In this way he had forged semi-secret cordial relations, ties of mutual understanding, with workmates and supervisors.

These factors and more converged to make PITA the target not so much of one man's crude comments as of an entire group's resentment, disdain, and hostility. What directly triggered her breakdown was nothing the Jerk said, but comments from two female co-workers on a hot summer day when jobs were being rotated. One called out so that all could hear, "I don't want to work with the cripple." The second, distributing sweatbands to combat the heat, passed PITA by, saying, "You don't work hard enough to get one."

Given the social dynamic in this workplace, it is easy to see why the higher-ups did nothing to rein the Jerk in. Addressing PITA's complaints would have meant taking on not just an individual harassing male but a cohesive group of male and female workers that was functioning productively in the overall organizational context. Each successive higher level of union or management authority to which PITA appealed was faced with challenging, disrupting, and overruling an even larger part of the organization. How much damage to morale and productivity can a senior official reasonably be expected to risk, for the sake of shielding one partially disabled woman from jokes other women laugh at?

"Even so," you may say, "somebody should have done something." This comment has been made in every case I know of Dr. PITA's elimination from a university faculty. It is a common exhortation of kind-hearted people working somewhere else. The common answer by people involved in the elimination process is, "You don't know what it's like to have to put up with her. If you think she's been treated so unfairly, why don't you give her a job? Meanwhile, get off my back."

17

The star chamber

In keeping with the times, many or most current cases of professorial elimination include accusations of sexual harassment. Sometimes, as in the factory-worker's case just described, a female Dr. PITA makes this charge against one or more of her eliminators. More often, a male Dr. PITA is himself accused. Cases of both kinds are commonly heard in a sexual-harassment tribunal.

This quasi-judicial body merits scrutiny here, as a new and valuable administrative resource. It may be deployed in Stage Three, as a mechanism for giving official definition to the critical incident, to Dr. PITA's misconduct, and to the requisite punishment. Alternatively, it may be brought into play by either side in Stage Four: the aftermath of the handling of the incident, consisting of appeals, grievances, protests, inquiries, and other manoeuvres toward resolving things. This point of the present guidebook, where attention begins to shift from the third to the fourth stage, is opportune for analyzing the place of this tribunal in contemporary academic organization.

Tribunals were rare in universities, even in government, until the 1960s. Until then, the bulk of decisions were made directly by executive and legislative bodies: elected officials in the case of government, or in the case of a university, by the board, senate, president, dean, and so on. Occasionally, decisions of the responsible officials became issues of debate among lawmakers and the public, or were appealed to the courts.

Tribunals have changed how decisions are made. At base, they are part of the overall rationalization process, the organization of life in more complex, intricate ways for more efficient achievement of specific goals. The logic behind them is that instead of leaving decisions to overburdened and inexpert governments (administrations) and legislatures (senates), it is better to delegate decisions according to subject area to subordinate bodies that have the time and expertise necessary to render them wisely. By now, tribunals have proliferated to the point of spawning a major specialty in law schools, administrative law.

Whatever the tribunal at issue, whether a municipal board on land-use planning or a university committee for dispensing research funds, the key legal point is that it derives its authority from that of the body or official who establishes it and appoints its members. It can act only on matters within its jurisdiction, as spelled out in an enabling statute: some kind of law or policy.

The tribunal of interest here is commonly called the Ethics Committee or the Sexual and Racial Harrassment Committee. Most universities created one in the late 1970s or early 1980s, when concerns about male predation upon women loomed large in public opinion, capably voiced by authors like Catherine MacKinnon, Andrea Dworkin, and Constance Backhouse. In some universities, the tribunal's mandate was limited to sexual harassment and abuse. In most, it was defined more broadly to include prejudice or discrimination against other kinds of victim, or even "unethical behaviour" in general.

Typical policies provide that the committee have five to ten members, with equal representation of faculty, staff, and students. Commonly, though not at Waterloo, a staff member with the title of Harassment Officer is employed to administer the policy in its informal aspects and attend to the correct handling of formal complaints.

Every administrator should study the enabling statute for the ethics tribunal in his or her institution, since it may differ somewhat from the one at Waterloo, which I use for illustration here. At Waterloo, although the senate approved the enabling policy, the tribunal derives its authority effectively from the office of the Vice-President, Academic, & Provost, whom the policy cites explicitly fourteen times. The UW Ethics Committee is an extension of his office. He holds its leash. He appoints its six members and decides which one shall be its chair. The outcome of any formal hearing is a recommendation made to him, which he may reject or accept and implement. According to the policy, either complainant or respondent in a formal proceeding can appeal the provost's decision to the president. The policy provides for no further appeal.

The ethics tribunal is sometimes decried as a star chamber, as if this were something to be ashamed of. In fact, the Court of Star Chamber dispensed a great deal of justice in England in the sixteenth and early seventeenth centuries. It was established for honourable purposes not unlike those prompting the creation of university ethics committees in our own time. The name comes simply from the room where the court convened, and has no more significance than if Waterloo's ethics tribunal were informally called the Court of Needles 3043.

The problem in England at the time was that the common-law courts were often prevented from enforcing the law by corruption—what might today be called old-boy networks. The Crown therefore established the Star Chamber as a "prerogative court." That meant it was identified with the royal executive power and answerable only to the highest authority, much as the ethics tribunal is an arm of the provost's authority. Thereby the influence of local nobles and gentry was reduced. In a similar way, the ethics tribunal circumvents the influence of professors behaving as petty feudal lords.

Similarities of today's ethics tribunal to the Star Chamber of old do not end there. It operates for the most part secretly, so that public pressure cannot interfere with the judgments handed down. Juries are not called upon, decisions being made instead by people appointed by the highest authority. The ethics tribunal is not bound by the procedural niceties of common law, as these are observed even today in public courts, but can be as flexible in how cases are handled as circumstances recommend. Proceedings may be commenced not just at a complainant's request, as in a civil suit, but on the basis of information received from third parties. Like the Star Chamber, the ethics tribunal is not burdened by the safeguards to individual liberty that can make conviction of an obviously guilty party difficult. Finally, while its punishments are arbitrary, they stop short of dismissal from the university, much as the Star Chamber had authority to fine, imprison, and pillory, but not to put anyone to death.

When Thomas Cardinal Wolsey was chancellor of England in the early sixteenth century, he expanded use of the Star Chamber. Anything that could be considered a breach of the peace was a suitable basis on which to convene the court. Wolsey urged, moreover, that complainants approach the Star Chamber first, instead of waiting to be disappointed by the courts of common law.

In a strikingly similar manner, the jurisdiction of harassment tribunals at Waterloo and elsewhere has stretched over time to embrace almost anything deemed unethical. The first principle of Waterloo's policy requires:

> That each member of the University endeavour to contribute to the existence of a just and supportive community based on equality and respect for individual differences.

No complaint can escape an umbrella clause like this, unless the tribunal decides to let it go. As in Wolsey's time, the tribunal increasingly deals with complaints from the start, without waiting to see if department chairs or deans can resolve them according to old "common-law" traditions.

Harassment tribunals are thus situated to perform the same role in today's universities as the Court of Star Chamber did in the maturity of its final decades: to wrest power away from lower-level authorities (nobles or professors) and transfer it case by case to the central authority (the Crown or senior management). All that is necessary is that appointments to the tribunal be made with care, to ensure that all the members—faculty, staff, and students—have strong loyalty to senior management and share in the vibrant team spirit that makes the university a functioning, coherent whole. If the committee is appropriately staffed, senior management can let it operate quite independently—at arm's length, to use the common phrase—and still be confident of decisions in its favour.

I am aware of but one case (others undoubtedly exist) where such a tribunal delivered a verdict greatly at odds with senior management's preference. In that case, the tribunal heard charges of sexual misconduct against Dr. PITA, found him guilty of no offense, and therefore recommended punishments that stopped short of dismissal. Sorely disappointed by the tribunal's lenience, the responsible administrator sent the tribunal chair a sharp letter of reprimand.

In all the other ethics or harassment cases against Dr. PITA in my study, the tribunal and senior management displayed confluence of judgment. The reason is clear. You may recall the frustration of the administrator quoted near the start of this book, over "troublemakers who know how to go just so far and no farther." Behind the closed doors of the star chamber, going "just so far" is enough to be found guilty. Procedures are flexible enough to prevent troublemakers from making an escape. Dr.

PITA can dispute jurisdiction, quote policies, and cite rules of natural justice all he wants (a wise committee allows him ample time). Then the tribunal makes its own interpretation and hands down the judgment he deserves.

But what if Dr. PITA herself approaches the tribunal with an ethics or harassment charge? I know of seven cases of this kind, four involving accusations of abuse on the basis of gender, two on the basis of race, and one on the basis of both gender and race. Six of the seven cases never reached the point of a formal hearing. Either the tribunal ruled it lacked jurisdiction to hear the case, or Dr. PITA gave up after months of run-around (more properly called attempts at informal resolution). In the one case that was formally heard, the committee ruled that Dr. PITA had misinterpreted the actions of those seeking her elimination, that their motives had nothing to do with gender or sex.

It does not really matter how strongly you, as an individual, are aligned with the forces of zero tolerance. The point here is more basic: that a properly staffed ethics tribunal is as powerful a device for corralling undesirables and promoting peace in the university as the Court of Star Chamber was in the England of Henry VIII. It is true that the Star Chamber was abolished by the Long Parliament in 1641, as part of a democratizing trend. No such trend is likely to surface in today's universities, so long as the job market in most academic fields remains as tight as now.

18

Making the star chamber work

So that this book may be of maximum practical value, this chapter sets forth in point form some helpful hints for the professors, secretaries, and students who sit on harassment tribunals. Not being professional administrators, these people may lack managerial sophistication. Whoever appoints them will do well to provide them with guidelines that will ensure the tribunal's effective operation.

These tips are for the modal situation, where the tribunal needs to bring down a finding of Dr. PITA's guilt and a recommendation for punishment. Cases where Dr. PITA herself appeals to the tribunal are easier to deal with, usually by finding a plausible way to rule her complaint out of jurisdiction.

These suggestions are based on the functioning of ethics and harassment committees in actual cases at Waterloo and elsewhere. Since policies differ somewhat among universities, these measures must not be applied mechanically but with due regard for the enabling statute in a given institution. Still, the functioning of such tribunals is quite similar across universities. I was surprised that a fictional depiction of a university ethics tribunal in 1996, on the popular TV sit-com *Third Rock from the Sun*, was a credible composite of actual cases in my study.

1. The tribunal should extend its jurisdiction or catchment area however broadly is required to take up the complaint against

Dr. PITA—whether the incident occurred on campus or off, in his professorial role or outside it.

2. Ideally, Dr. PITA should be found guilty of something before he finds out what it is. The Harassment Officer may assist one or more complainants in drawing up a plausible preliminary indictment for subsequent approval by the tribunal as a whole.

3. To enlist Dr. PITA's cooperation in his own undoing, confound the roles of counsellor, prosecutor, and judge. In conversations with an official he believes is being friendly, he may make incriminating statements that can later be held against him.

4. Make sure the victim-accuser is on side. More than one case has been lost, even with many ardent complainants, because the alleged victim did not herself find Dr. PITA's behaviour objectionable.

5. Reward accusers. For lowly undergraduates, the attentions of important university officials may be reward enough. Financial compensation or revision of grades, on account of injuries sustained, may also be considered.

6. Avoid falsifiable statements in the indictment. Vagueness and innuendo are far more effective than charges that lend themselves to being disproven.

7. Once the decision is made to proceed to a formal hearing, move as quickly as possible, showing a sense of great urgency. A hearing that cannot be arranged promptly may not be able to be arranged at all.

8. Ignore Dr. PITA's lawyer, if he has one, and forbid the lawyer's presence at the hearing. Explain that domestic tribunals of a university proceed by norms of collegiality, and that legalistic, adversarial measures are out of place.

9. If the faculty association or other bodies attempt to intervene on Dr. PITA's behalf, accuse them of trying to exert undue influence. Insist that the tribunal will not bend to the political pressure being applied.

10. Ignore claims that the tribunal is biased against him. Respond as one chair did: "I am satisfied that this committee member has no apprehension of bias."

11. Disregard evidence in Dr. PITA's favour on substantive grounds. Describe it as irrelevant or not germane to the issues under consideration.

12. Disregard evidence in Dr. PITA's favour on procedural grounds. Say it was submitted at the wrong time, to the wrong official, or in the wrong format.

13. If there is evidence that Dr. PITA has discussed the case outside the tribunal (he may admit, for instance, having talked about it with his wife, his dean, or some colleagues), charge him with breach of confidentiality.

14. If Dr. PITA speaks his accusers' names outside the tribunal, charge him with breach of confidentiality and with attempting to damage their reputations and cause them to suffer.

15. If Dr. PITA (or his colleague-advisor, if the policy provides for one) objects to the tribunal's procedures, remind him that this is not a court of law, that collegiality must be insisted upon, and that the tribunal will not entertain editorial comments.

16. Ignore the references to context that Dr. PITA is almost sure to make. Explain that the tribunal's only concern is with this particular incident, not with what may have happened before or after.

17. Find an excuse to make a confidential investigation that may yield additional complaints and is useful in any case for damaging Dr. PITA's reputation. Contact former students, for example, or advertise in the newspaper. In a case against a policeman pita, the tribunal set out to contact each of the 2,047 women he had had something to do with during his eight years on the force.

18. Try to provoke Dr. PITA into losing his temper or doing something rash, then make appropriate additional charges.

Like most professors, Dr. PITA is so proud and vain that the hearing itself will insult and fluster him.

19. In the report at the end, find Dr. PITA guilty of something, even if it is not what he was initially charged with. The important thing is to find against him. The precise nature of the finding is of secondary importance.

20. Write a long report, preferably at least ten pages single-spaced. Number sections and paragraphs. Include lots of footnotes. Be vague and repetitive. Include nothing that could be quoted out of context as being in Dr. PITA's favour.

21. Recommend multiple punishments: for example, requirements to make several different apologies, go for counselling, and attend a series of workshops, in addition to a financial penalty.

22. Do not let your animus against Dr. PITA show, nor lead you to write things that are obviously untrue. Senior managers will not take kindly to a report so extreme they are obliged to reject it, and may deny you the rewards you will otherwise receive for your service to the university.

23. The report should include innuendo so damaging to Dr. PITA that he will not himself release it publicly, however strong his objections. Suggestions of sexual predation or mental unbalance serve well.

24. Do not release the report publicly, lest the tribunal be revealed as a kanagaroo court. After my first ethics hearing, the provost put the report on the Internet. I understand from him that he now regrets that decision.

25. For the same reason, never release audio-tapes of the proceeding, much less a transcript. If this cannot be avoided (in connection with an appeal, for instance), Dr. PITA may be allowed to listen to the tapes under administrative supervision, but under no circumstances should he be allowed to walk away with a copy.

19

Managing moral panic

Fire is the best metaphor for understanding it. It can burn you in a flash. Out of control, it consumes everything. To be near it is risky. Failing to notice it can mean losing your life. Managed well, it gives the power of Prometheus.

It is passionate, collective craving to get rid of someone in order to ease anxiety and fear, and make everything right again. *Mass hysteria* it may be called, or sometimes *zealotry, mob violence, witch-hunt, lynching,* or the *rule of crowds.* A classic sociological label is *moral panic.*

You may have said at some time that moral panic has no place in a university, that here intellect controls emotion, reason rules passion, sobriety prevents frenzy, intellectual independence subverts conformity, and multicausal science disallows singlemindedness. This is the myth academe turns on. As an administrator, you have a duty to proclaim and defend the myth. You do not need to believe it.

To succeed in your job (and keep from getting burned), you need to see through the academic veil as Fergal Keane did in Rwanda, when he interviewed the vice-rector of Butare. Keane has already gagged on the stench of unburied bodies in decay, but he knows better than to expect open fire in the university. The vice-rector speaks impeccable English and French. His clothes are spotless. He is too sophisticated to blurt out his feelings.

He is a man of such cleverness that he has contrived not to see any of the tens of thousands who have been killed in and around Butare. Nor has he heard any screams of dying people. But he is wondering now what will happen.

Moral panic is more than a collective push to humiliate or expel members of a group, so that the rest may carry on happily. It is more than good apples joining stems to throw bad apples from the barrel, before their rot spreads. It is that plus fire: a fury, free of doubt, to get the unpleasantness over with. Moral panic is in the present tense. The future and the past be damned. We do this now.

Thad Snow called it an elemental thing, an impressive human experience that enables "all good people not only to believe the fantastic and improbable, but also to forget or ignore the obvious and well-known." Harry Truman put it this way:

You read your history and you'll see that from time to time people in every country have seemed to lose their good sense, got hysterical, and got off the beam. I don't know what gets into people.

Whatever it is, it gets into academics, too. In *The House of Seven Gables*, Hawthorne draws a lesson from the execution of the alleged witch, Matthew Maule:

It should teach us, among its other morals, that the influential classes, and those who take upon themselves to be leaders of the people, are fully liable to all the passionate error that has ever characterized the maddest mob.

Hawthorne is right, though his word *error* says more than the managerial point of view finds necessary. Is it error if no one ever knows? If the Salem witch trials were not the subject of so many books, would they have been a mistake? If the Nazis had won the war, would their secret elimination of Jews and other undesirables have been wrong? If Thomas More had not been canonized and heroized by critics of the Crown, might his death have been deserved? Nobody knows what Ms. PITA has been through in the factory these many years. No authority has found it wrong. Administratively, the saving grace of workplace eliminations is that most of them stay in the closet of routine decision-making. In the press report after Billy Budd was hanged, so Melville writes, he was described as your average mutineer.

To greater or less degree, moral panic fuels the effort to rid your academic unit of Dr. PITA. His name implies as much, and the times encourage it. Your ethics tribunal, if it is staffed by true believers in its aims, is a tinderbox of hysteria. Created to stamp out specific kinds of misconduct, the tribunal encourages single-issue obsessions and an unbalanced, moralistic mentality. It can ignite even sodden minds and set them raging in righteous indignation.

As an administrator, you should manage the panic, not fight it. People's anger is real, and they need outlets for it. Standing in the way of a crowd is the stuff of which ex-provosts are made. Your task is to lead, not obstruct. You distance yourself from the one on whom mud is thrown, lest you yourself be targetted. You keep your clothes spotless.

Equally important, you yourself do not throw mud. You leave dirty work to students, secretaries, and professors with hot heads. You stifle or conceal your own blood lust. Your part of the process is to channel others' passion so as to normalize Dr. PITA's removal from good company: to cite precedents that make it seem reasonable, to enact procedures that resemble due process, and to avoid giving the impression that you make up rules as you go along.

As I recount one case of moral panic managed by a president, put yourself in his shoes. What might you have done differently? The Dr. PITA at issue was a man of colour, tenured for twenty years, early fifties in age, popular in the classroom, with the rank of full professor. His back had been bitten informally for years. He seemed most at home in the intellectual world of his country of origin, in whose traditional garb he sometimes showed up for class.

In the fall of 1994, a student complained to the dean that Dr. PITA had sexually assaulted her that summer. Here at last was a serious incident! The specific charge was that in a gathering of students on a field trip in a tent, he had touched her for a prurient purpose and some days later kissed her. She had let him know that his attentions were unwelcome, and he did not persist. Still, the victim wanted Dr. PITA fired. So did her fellow students, who both vouched for her honesty and disputed Dr. PITA's financial probity. The dean, along with sundry professors and students, saw the case as a test of whether the university's anti-harassment policy had teeth. The dean formally dismissed Dr. PITA for unethical behaviour and suspended him without pay, as provided in the tenure policy, until his appeal of the elimination decision could be heard.

Dr. PITA's appeal landed on the president's desk months later. The decision confronting him was delicate. On one side was a passionate movement that wanted PITA gone. The chief eliminator was a dean, an enraged group of students and faculty was mobilized, and a victim was grieving loudly and crying for justice.

On the other side was the professor, who refused to resign, whose health did not fail for one full year, and who was making a spirited defense. He claimed the accusations against him were malicious and false. His alleged misconduct had occurred two continents away and outside university auspices. Further, the official finding of his guilt had not been made by a court or even a university tribunal, but only by a dean. Indeed, Dr. PITA had sought a hearing before the ethics tribunal, but the dean had jumped the gun on it, arguing that the case was too serious to await action by a tribunal normally restricted to lesser offenses.

The case was still formally secret as the president began to act. Gossip had more or less destroyed Dr. PITA's reputation among his colleagues and students, and suspension from teaching had isolated him from classrooms where he might have started rebuilding it, but the dean's finding against him had not been publicly reported. Dr. PITA himself had insisted that all proceedings be confidential, and his request had been formally honoured.

The president bungled his first attempt to manage the panic in this case. In a confidential judgment, he agreed with the victim. It was clear, he later wrote,

> from my interviews with the complainants that the student's story, when told to the group, was found credible and believed by the others. I too found her to be credible and accepted her recollection of the events.

Nonetheless, the president ruled that Dr. PITA's misconduct was not so serious as to warrant dismissal. He ordered him to resume teaching for the fall term of 1995, but with a fine of six months' salary, to be deducted from his paycheques on a pro-rated basis over the next two years. Dr. PITA would be permitted to appeal this judgment to an arbitrator. In that event, the university would seek his dismissal.

This resolution only fanned the crowd's zeal to have Dr. PITA expelled, and his resolve never to submit or yield. Protesting his innocence as before, PITA appealed to the arbitrator. A hearing date was set for late October. The university lawyers pieced together their case. The victim, her supporters, and the dean were fired up to testify in the arbitrator's quasi-court. Prior findings of guilt by dean and president bolstered their case.

During the last two weeks of October, the president was almost undone. The combined stress of reduced income, teaching in a climate of hostile whispering, and preparing his case to the arbitrator overtaxed Dr. PITA's strength. A heart ailment landed him in hospital. On October 18, he wrote the president a letter withdrawing his appeal and acquiescing to the fine, but still protesting his innocence. He pledged to continue in his position, and

> to serve my students and colleagues at the university in the best ways possible to enhance the reputation of the university in accordance with the highest ethical standards.

The cancellation of the hearing, a degradation ceremony they had looked forward to, enraged Dr. PITA's would-be eliminators. On October 27, thirty students crashed a meeting of the dean with the university lawyer, expressing disgust at the leniency of the six-month fine and demanding Dr. PITA's ouster. Their outrage now extended to the president. Why had he gone soft? If he believed the victim's accusations, why had he lacked the courage to impose her requested penalty? The old boys' network must have reared its head. Further horror: the student newspaper had been forewarned of the protest and had sent in photographers. The next issue (November 3) would have banner headlines. How would the president look?

This Stage-Four development in Dr. PITA's case underscores the advice offered earlier: never stand in the way of a crowd. Do not fight a panic; manage it. In this case, the president got the message in the nick of time.

The protest occurred on a Thursday. By the following Monday, October 30, the president had thrown confidentiality to the wind and made public to the world a detailed account of the incident. He reported Dr. PITA's transgressions in detail: that "he had breached his obligations to adhere to reasonable and proper directions from his Dean," "committed unwanted touching," failed to provide the participants in the field trip with a financial account, fondled a student and later kissed her on the mouth. Yet, so the president protested in his own defense, Dr. PITA's misconduct was not so serious as to warrant dismissal. The fondling had occurred in a setting where "others were present and able to come to the student's assistance had Dr. PITA not desisted." A suspension from teaching had already been imposed, and now the fine. The president reported himself "satisfied that Dr. PITA posed no threat of further behaviour of this sort towards students."

With cleverness enough to make Pontius Pilate grin, the university newspaper then scooped the student press. On November 1, it published the full text of the president's statement, along with—one might say this was the master stroke—Dr. PITA's photograph. City newspapers and a national magazine picked up the story.

The student newspaper came through as expected on November 3, with a multipage spread. The "campus question" of the week was, "What do you think is the appropriate penalty for a professor who sexually assaults one of their students?" Wholesome-looking lads and lasses were pictured, with answers like these:

Termination of tenure. No question...out of here.

Totally prohibited from teaching here ever again.

Trash them, get rid of them, we don't need them anymore.

A public hanging.

Dr. PITA could no longer show his face on campus. He applied for medical leave but was turned down. With strong administrative encouragement, he then took early retirement.

One of the most important insights in Anne Llewellyn Barstow's book *Witchcraze*, a study of the panic that swept Europe in the sixteenth and seventeenth centuries, is how the elimination of the witches reinforced the transfer of power occurring at that time from local communities to states. She points out that in the main, the climate of zealotry and intolerance had its origin not in the common people but in the rulers. Governments were becoming more efficient and centralized. Popular hysteria served to strengthen state authority.

Royal agents asserted their influence in parts of Europe never before interfered with. They demanded not only taxes and military levies but also a new ideological conformity.... Secular courts took over prosecution of sexual crimes, matters formerly reserved for judgment in the more private sphere of church or neighborhood.

The moral panics currently afoot in universities can serve the similar purpose of strengthening the authority of senior management, and encouraging the ideological conformity necessary for universities to serve their function in a complex, globalized economic order. Moral panic is an administrator's best friend. The key point is to manage it.

20

October 19, 1997

Today, Sunday, I look back with relief on three productive weeks of work and forward to more weeks of it ahead. Like any worker, a writer gains momentum and loses it. For now I have it, thank God.

If the momentum lasts two weeks more, the book should be done, except for notes and polishing. The Outside Judge is still cooperating. No report from him again this week. I will fax him respectfully tomorrow.

This week's university newspaper reports that the provost has imposed a levy of one percent on departmental budgets across the university for the current fiscal year. In this way he aims to cut $1.3 million from the current operating budget, leaving it at $177.6 million.

Part of the reason for the midyear revision, so the paper says, is that the line for audit and legal fees has risen from $210,000 to $360,000. This increase, though the paper does not say so, is from the pita cases being fought in court: three that I know of this fiscal year.

My case will boost the item by thousands more if the Outside Judge rules in my favour. I have asked for reimboursement of my legal costs over the past four years, plus a year's research leave to compensate me for time lost. If the Outside Judge rules against me, the provost can rest easy. The

100

amount the university will save by not paying me for a month should cover the Outside Judge's fee.

The provost has never said for which month he intends to suspend me. I am on sabbatical leave until the first of January. Can a professor be suspended from a leave? The provost has said he won't suspend me during a teaching term, lest my services in the classroom be lost. Then what am I being suspended from? Writing letters of recommendation for students? Writing books like this? Reading books? The intended suspension looks to me like a fine, but labour law forbids that. Whom God wishes to destroy, he first makes mad.

Do you wonder what all this is about: why a university would devote so much time and energy to getting rid of a professor like me? If the hours were counted up, the task has consumed $.5 or $1 million of administrative time, and it has reduced my devotion to normal academic work by about three quarters for the past four years.

Cases of professorial elimination are similar in form. That is why I can outline a five-stage process and identify standard tactics and techniques. In this respect, Dr. PITA really is a single being of varying outward appearance. He is cross-cultural and trans-historical, and I am but one of his myriad embodiments.

Yet every Dr. PITA is as unique as the situation from which he should be expelled. In a case more transparent than most, a psychologist pita defied the learning-disabilities bureaucracy at his university in 1988.

Every year I receive ever more bizarre requests from students who claim that their poor academic performance is due to "learning disabilities" which they have inherited from their parents.

So began this pita's frontal attack in the campus newspaper. He concluded by proposing that students whose final grades reflect special accommodation of their alleged disabilities should have this warning appended to their transcripts:

The marks of this transcript were obtained with the help of the Office of Counselling and Career Development Services for Disabled Students. The fact that this student cannot write in proper English, i. e. that he is merely semi-literate, is due to brain damage or cerebral malfunctioning and should not be taken as a pretext for not hiring him, be it as an English professor, teacher or journalist.

Dr. PITA's article drew fire. The debate went on for months and grew to include three dozen passionate letters and articles in campus media, not counting articles in academic journals. The chair of Dr. PITA's department, the principal of his college, and the president of his university were among those writing in defense of the human rights code and the local disabilities office. Their contributions had an air of heartfelt apology for any discouragement learning-disabled students might have suffered as a result of seeing Dr. PITA's views in print.

Dr. PITA tangled administratively with his dean over the same issue, rebuffing pressure to give a passing grade to a low-achieving student with a certified disability.

On top of these disagreements was the fact that this Dr. PITA is German-born and multilingual, speaks with an accent, is married to a French woman, and displays in his personal comportment a formality and directness more often associated with Prussia than English Canada. He is good-humoured but not light-hearted. A childhood spent amidst the destruction, death and famine of World War II has left him with a seriousness about life uncommon among the children of postwar prosperity in North America.

In the spring of 1991, students in one of Dr. PITA's classes complained of sexual harassment. The dean and college head took the complaint very seriously and allowed it to balloon into a major incident that consumed Dr. PITA's life for an extended period—"Two Years in Kafkaland," he has called it—before he was cleared of wrongdoing and the elimination effort turned back.

This feisty Dr. PITA made his troubles public from the start, and his case has been widely discussed. Yet the accounts I have seen gloss over the key connection between the dispute over learning disabilities in 1988, and the elimination process formally begun in 1991. The case is generally understood simply as a regrettable instance of a professor being falsely charged with sexual harassment.

Alleged sexual harassment was no more the heart of this psychologist pita's case than of the case of the factory-worker pita described earlier. In a different cultural climate, he would have been charged with heresy, communism, or advocacy of interracial marriage. By the time the charges were made, the first two stages of the elimination process had been carried out. Informally, he had already been removed from respectable company, and symbolically positioned on the opposite side of the fence from the authorities in his workplace.

What makes the process of professorial elimination so hard to make sense of is that the issues on which a case nominally turns rarely coincide with the "real" ones. It is usually in the interests of the eliminators to obscure the "real" reasons for their collective action. These are often best left unspoken, without even a denial. Students who mobilized against a foreign-accented Dr. PITA at a Quebec university in the 1970s, and plastered the campus with posters denouncing him, did themselves no favour by the line at the bottom: "This has nothing to do with the fact that he is a Jew." A successful elimination effort often proceeds with no reference to what explains it best.

Yet participants should keep themselves conscious of what the real reasons are, lest they be duped by their own fabrications. Exactly how does this professor threaten collective well-being? Which of the group's sacred cows does Dr. PITA touch? By which

measure of collegiality in this particular context does PITA fall
short? If the administrators in the psychologist's case had kept
answers to these questions clearer in their minds, they might have
been able to achieve their objective, instead of muddling clumsily
about and eventually suffering the indignity of his public
exoneration.

What my own case is really about is the articles, lectures,
letters and memos I wrote about my home university, its character
and mode of governance, during the eight years leading up to the
incident of 1993.

Even now just forty years old, Waterloo is a very special
university, and I would not wish to have spent the past quarter-
century anywhere but here. It was founded on explicit rejection of
the ivory-tower traditions that prevent most older institutions
from addressing the world as it is. Year after year Waterloo tops
the *Macleans* reputational ranking of Canadian universities. What
makes us the "overall best" is the same as what made Salamanca
best in sixteenth-century Spain, or Harvard best in nineteenth-
century America: resonance with cultural trends and close ties to
rising elites. Waterloo likes to think of itself as the MIT of the
north, on the cutting edge of computer-based technologies and
the other kinds of knowledge today's global economic order
craves.

Yet during the 1980s I came to believe that Waterloo was
losing the perspective and independence essential to any
university, that we were breaking our academic vows to students,
the public, and the pursuit of truth, and becoming the whore of
big business. Nothing seemed to matter here except training
employees for large corporations and doing research that would
bolster some company's bottom line. The market mentality
seemed to have permeated campus culture so much that the
larger purposes of life were escaping notice. Decision-making
seemed to have slipped away from scholars into a clique of

technocrats more concerned with servicing corporations than with educating citizens.

Those were the kind of things I said in my contributions to campus debate, and I pressed for change in our way of doing things. My views were not socialist or radical. I said the kind of things financier George Soros said in his article in *Atlantic Monthly* last February: that large-scale private enterprise needs to be controlled, that competitive individualism is undermining the common good, and that the spread of market values into aspects of life where they do not belong is threatening democracy.

When I was invited in 1985 to take part in a campus lecture series, it was a chance to nail my theses to a conspicuous door. I said job training is too limited a goal for a university, no more adequate than the formerly touted goal of truth for truth's sake.

My purpose is to throw a plague on both these houses and to vote for a third alternative: practical eduation, but practical for living life dynamically, creatively, critically, wisely, in its entirety. Our students are indeed future employees, but they are more. They are heirs to this whole human experiment called Canada. ... Isn't this the best reason to try to make them aware of the flux that is life?

In his remarks after my lecture, the economist who had introduced me said I had bitten the hand that feeds me. He was right, and I bit it some more in subsequent years. Since 1993, the hand that feeds me has also been slapping me in the face. The dispute between our local administrators and me is not about sexism, racism, harassment, abuse, corruption, insensitivity, or any of the other nominal charges. It is about whether there is room here for an outspoken critic of academic subservience to corporate power and the marketization of life.

Waterloo's managers would be loath to agree with this portrayal of our dispute, just as those at the psychologist-Pita's university would not likely admit real reasons for the elimination process there. Such openness is not in their interests. I suspect, however, that the eliminators in both cases have been insufficiently conscious, even in the privacy of their minds, of their real motivation. Their rage has been too blind. This has so far prevented achievement of their objective in either the psychologist's case or mine.

Stage Four

Aftermath of the Incident

In retrospect, what perhaps troubles me most is that my occasional spells of uneasiness during this period were concerned mainly with the direction I was taking as an architect, with my growing estrangement from Tessenow's doctrines. On the other hand I must have had the feeling that it was no affair of mine when I heard the people around me declaring an open season on Jews, Freemasons, Social Democrats, or Jehovah's Witnesses. I thought I was not implicated if I myself did not take part.

Albert Speer, *Inside the Third Reich*, 1969;
Hitler's personal architect, Speer was also
Minister of Armaments from 1942 until the end
of the war; he was convicted of war crimes at
Nuremberg and served a sentence of 20 years.

21

No playful romp

Before reviewing manoeuvres the two sides may make in the penultimate stage of Dr. PITA's elimination, a reminder is in order: this process is no playful romp. It is as serious and grand as the bullfight or the hunt, only subtler.

The normal stuff of a university is research, teaching, study and dialogue. What is said matters more than who says it. Self takes second place to truth. Every story has more sides than two. Base instincts are repressed in favour of high ideals. The university is a City on a Hill, more than Winthrop's Massachusetts could ever hope to be.

You not only voice this myth but know there is truth in it. Sometimes—in a lab, library, lecture-hall or seminar-room—minds meet where they have never met before. It happens more often than administrators know. When it does, one counts the university a holy place.

Yet the city's boundaries meander down the hill into a swamp, which is also part of it, and it is there that professorial elimination takes place. Necessary though the process may be, it is so exceptional that those involved may behave as if in a colloquium.

I have been present at the commencement of so far three dismissal hearings before an arbitrator. Each took place in a well-appointed meeting room with a single table in the centre, around

which scholars might on other occasions sit and reason together.
I knew each pita well enough to have tasted his terror. Watching
him shake hands and exchange pleasantries with his eliminators,
introduce himself to the arbitrator ("No, I'm not the university
lawyer, I'm the professor being dismissed"), and find a seat at the
table, I marvelled at how high and cool the manners were,
compared to how low and hot the purposes.

Professorial elimination is about the crushing of an
individual by a group. It is the sort of phenomenon that makes
sociology's basic tenet believable: that a group is more than the
sum of its members, that it is a fact *sui generis*. The contest is not
Drs. A, B, and C on one side, Dr. P on the other. It is ABC
University casting an outcast out. The aim is to take away from
Dr. PITA whatever of ABC university he has within him—or
sometimes even, whatever he has of academic life. One arbitrator,
upholding a decision to dismiss for unethical behaviour, wrote in
his report that he

> would not shrink from concluding that a person so uncaring
> of the interests of the two institutions, from which he
> knowingly withheld vital information, has proved himself unfit
> to hold a tenured appointment at any university.

There is a gesture that tells what is going on. One pita
after another reported it to me. Then I came across a literary
reference to it from G. K. Chesterton. He was discussing Charles
Dickens, the man who made a hero of Oliver Twist. Dickens
disliked, according to G.K.C., "a certain look on the face of a
man when he looks down on another man." Chesterton added
that "that look on that face is the only thing that we have really
to fight between here and the fires of hell."

Dickens and Chesterton, idealists both, were enraptured
with the hill but despised the swamp that is also part of every city
of man, including the university. The point is this: that in most
cases of professorial elimination, there comes a moment when Dr.

PITA's eyes catch the countenance of the chief eliminator or some other honoured member of the group, and the latter smiles—or grins or smirks or snickers. The look is not always intentional. Often it seems to be an involuntary eruption of pleasure, an irrepressible bodily sign of satisfaction that the deed is done: that the collective has successfully withdrawn what life it can from one who does not belong.

Pictures of this awe-inspiring look hold morbid fascination, and appear often on TV, as when Canadian peace-keepers posed with the Somali boy they had beaten to death. In print media, the most accessible pictures of the smile are from records of Reserve Police Battalion 101, a German unit responsible for exterminating Jews in Poland in 1942-43. The soldiers often grinned for the camera in postures of dominance over those they were exterminating. Reproduced in at least two popular books, these pictures show the same look many undesirable professors recall seeing on the face of an eliminator. That, of course, is the extent of the comparison. When academic managers oust Dr. PITA from a tenured professorship, they are not taking away her life or freedom, anti-Semitism is rarely a factor, and the number of people involved is small.

Even so, an adequate analysis has to recognize the tremendous undertaking workplace exclusion is. There is no other way to understand the many steps the parties may take in Stage Four. All of Dr. PITA's life may not be at stake, but a good part of it is. Discussing this phenomenon once with a professor originally from eastern Europe, I remarked upon our good fortune in North America, in contrast to his homeland during the Stalinist era, where professors not uncommonly were put to death. "Yes," he answered, "but in the Anglo-Saxon world, people have a way of sucking your blood without breaking the skin."

22

Unit-think

Stigma is not lightly borne, and Dr. PITA will probably fight it with whatever resources she can draw upon, trying to keep her case open and on the administrative agenda. She and her supporters may appeal to an arbitrator, file a court action, petition the board of governors, or seek publicity to correct what they see as a miscarriage of justice.

You, as an administrator, try to keep the case closed. You want to move on to important issues crowding your agenda. You will not second-guess the painful decision that has been made. Instead of nursing old wounds, you want the period of healing to begin. Nor do you want to waste scarce resources on a matter that has already taken too much of too many people's time.

A striking difference in mood separates later from earlier stages of an elimination process. Until the objective has been achieved, the group is in an animated state, alive with verbal and emotional activity. Loyal citizens let their minds dwell on the problem at length, they huddle in small groups to share rumours, they write letters to the editor demanding action, they organize meetings, sign statements of collective solidarity, and put up posters. Once the movement has successfully decommissioned its target, to quote Thad Snow, "those who have been swept into its vortex recover promptly and thereafter prefer to forget all about it." In the university, once Dr. PITA has been formally dismissed or placed in some kind of doghouse, those who have been preoccupied with this unpleasant task eagerly return to routine concerns.

Whether an elimination decision can be maintained in the face of PITA's efforts to have it overturned depends utterly on the cohesiveness of the academic unit. The referent here is probably the university as a whole, since the formal action against PITA will ordinarily have been taken by senior management, or at least approved at that level. Stage Four then becomes a matter of circling the various wagons of the institution in order to keep PITA outside and prevent her reentry into respectable company.

Psychologist Irving Janis made the classic analysis of the required cohesiveness, calling it *groupthink*, a term I avoid here because of its negative connotations. I would rather call it *unit-think*, a word that, when pronounced with some Central European accent, sounds like *unity*, without which no organization can survive. Janis recognizes the positive effects of concurrence-seeking in organizations, notably for boosting morale and surviving crises, but he plays them down. Perhaps because of his own immersion in a culture of individual rights, he associates high cohesiveness with poor decision-making. His book is an analysis of four fiascoes of U.S. foreign policy (the Bay of Pigs invasion, for example), each of which he attributes to "groupthink" among the decision-makers.

Janis may be right with respect to complex matters of war and national defense, but what he calls the "Groupthink Syndrome" is exactly what the successful cases of professorial elimination in my study display. The matter of Dr. PITA is not especially complex among the decisions administrators face. It is not like designing a new degree program or piecing together a project of interdisciplinary research. It is a matter of removing one crooked tree from a forest of upright trees. The more the parties involved cooperate, the quicker the job will get done.

Your blood is not icewater. You do not enjoy other people's pain. You know that the PITA decision is what Janis calls a hardhearted one. You are sorry for that. Still, what matters now is as he says, "remaining loyal to the group by sticking with the decisions to which the group has committed itself," even if certain consequences "disturb the conscience of the members." Janis offers as the central theme of his analysis that the more esprit-de-corps is achieved in a decision-making group, the more unit-think takes over, increasing the likelihood of dehumanizing conduct toward out-groups. In this case the out-group is Dr. PITA, a professor to whom such conduct has to be applied, because she is threatening the group. Without unit-think, the effort may fail.

The following eight indicators of unit-think are adapted from Janis's research. To the extent that they apply to your academic unit, it can be expected to hold firm to the decisions already taken in the PITA case.

- A strong, even unquestioned belief that the members of your academic unit have integrity and high ethical standards, that they are not nasty people.
- A high degree of optimism and acceptance of risk in your unit, because people feel good about themselves.
- Quick discounting of warnings or new information that call into question decisions about PITA already made.
- A shared conviction that trying to debate or negotiate with PITA or her surrogates is a waste of time.
- Strong group pressure brought to bear on any professor or administrator who suggests backing down from decisions already made.
- An appearance of unanimity on this issue, any doubters keeping quiet and letting their silence give consent.
- Self-censorship of doubts among faculty and administrators, on account of how strongly everybody knows the Chief Eliminator feels on this issue.

- The emergence of self-appointed defenders of the academic unit, people who say in effect, "Right or wrong, we have to see this through. The institution is under siege and deserves our full support."

The achievement of unit-think in a university, or in one of its constituent academic units, is no easy task, and I am familiar with some institutions where the likelihood of even an obviously undesirable professor being eliminated is quite low. They are old-fashioned schools out of step with the times, where values on critical, independent thought, academic freedom, tenure, and individual rights continue to hold sway. They are places where the archaic conception of a university, as a place embracing all fields of knowledge, is still contemplated. By combining Janis's insights with the conclusions of my own research, I see five conditions that lend themselves to the unit-think that is required to make a decision against Dr. PITA stick.

The academic unit needs to have a culture of being specialized and special, an unusual *kind* of department, faculty or university. The way of being special—exceptionally excellent teaching, a substantive area of specialized expertise, a distinctive methodological orientation, or particular value commitments—can draw faculty intellectually and emotionally together and enable them to dig in their collective heels behind tough decisions.

Scoring high in objective rankings of universities as published by *U.S. News & World Report* or *Macleans*, or in similar rankings for particular disciplines, bolsters collective self-esteem, what Janis calls a sense of invulnerability, that steels a group against backsliding and second thoughts.

A financial squeeze as a result of cuts in governmental funding or unexpected declines in enrollment can produce a siege mentality, the perception of an unsympathetic or hostile environment, that reduces tolerance of dissent and reinforces collective commitment to pull together.

Unit-think is encouraged by any kind of uniformity among faculty—ethnicity, class, religion, gender, regional homeland, credentials, or whatever—and especially if many have one or more degrees from the institution where they are now employed. Diversity of background breeds differences of opinion and weakens team-spirit.

Leadership that is forceful yet personal, domineering yet ingratiating, is essential to achieving unit-think: a leader who states an opinion at the start of discussion, who lets people know that he or she means business and remembers things, who displays and demands institutional loyalty, and who works very hard. An academic who is "just taking my turn" at administration, and who openly looks forward to returning to teaching and research, is an obstacle to unit-think.

Politics is the art of the possible, and so is academic administration. No chair, dean, provost or president should initiate the process of eliminating an undesirable professor unless a fair amount of unit-think can be counted on. Without it, the process may have to be aborted even in Stage Four, with possibly devastating consequences for the institution and those in charge of its administration.

23

PITA's internal appeals

Two routes are open to Dr. PITA, for attempting to escape punishment and regain respectability. He will probably try both. One is to appeal to authorities within the university that are not yet involved. The other is to invite parties outside the university to bring their infuence to bear toward getting the eliminative decision overturned. This chapter considers ploys of the first kind.

In most universities, policy allows the appeal of a decision by a lower-level administrator to successively higher levels in the chain of command. At Waterloo, a dismissal decision is made by the dean, in consultation with the provost, and it can then be appealed to the president. A lesser humiliation imposed by a department chair can be appealed up the line to dean, provost, and president.

An astute Chief Eliminator anticipates these appeals and informs higher-level officials before discipline is imposed. This is what consultation means. The object is to pull as many higher authorities as possible into the elimination movement at the start. This is best done discreetly, so that if they are later called upon to hear an appeal, they can do so with an air of independence.

A Chief Eliminator who feels "on shaky ground" may try to strong-arm superiors into supporting the discipline, and at the same time scare off appeals, by citing the superiors in the Stage-Three letter to Dr. PITA:

After consultation with the Deans of Science and Graduate Studies, also with the Vice-President, Academic, and the University Harassment Officer, as well as the Departmental Committee on Appointments and Tenure, I have decided.... This tactic is not recommended. Senior managers do not like to feel coerced by subordinates. If you inveigle them into supporting this decision, you may lose their support of later ones. To avoid misunderstanding, it is a good idea to run a draft of your letter by the higher-level managers before sending it to Dr. PITA.

If Stage Three has been executed properly, Dr. PITA's appeals to higher line authority in Stage Four are not a problem. As one president candidly said to him, on the occasion of rejecting his appeal of dismissal, "The department chair, dean, and vice-president are men of integrity and good faith. They are closer to the situation than I, and they have made their best judgment as to what measures are appropriate. How can you expect me to overrule them?"

It is not uncommon for Dr. PITA to ask some well-positioned friend—the dean of a different faculty, for instance, a former administrator, or a distinguished professor—to act as intermediary and make representations to whoever is handling an appeal. Such intervention can be foiled in at least two ways. The intermediary's request for a meeting can be refused with regret, on grounds that it would be improper while the formal appeal is underway. Alternatively, you can meet with the intermediary, listen to the arguments offered, and say you will take them under advisement. Nothing is gained by showing anger to Dr. PITA's delegates or telling them to mind their own business.

There are in every university, indeed in every workplace, well-intentioned but softhearted champions of the underdog who wince at seeing discipline imposed on anyone. Usually they are themselves marginal to the institution's functioning and they harp incessantly on academic freedom and due process. *Pita-proxies* is

a good name for them. They are suckers for tales of woe. PITA
will unburden herself endlessly on them and send them pleading
on her behalf to one administrator after another. The best thing
to do is listen to them patiently, letting their expressions of
concern flow in one ear and out the other. For them, losing
battles is probably nothing new.

Professors of this kind often find their way onto the
academic freedom & tenure committee of the faculty association.
Having despaired of making their names as researchers or
administrators, they console themselves by patronizing undesirable
professors, denouncing admnistrative cruelty and pontificating
about faculty rights. They should not cause skilled academic
managers to lose sleep. In the university as in business and
industry, unions and similar employee associations are in the main
a refuge for workers who would like to be managers but do not
have what it takes. Putting up with their hectoring is a cross real
managers have to bear. It is sometimes possible to tap the faculty
association leadership for managerial talent, typically at the level
of department chair.

If a moral panic is underway, the faculty association is
likely to be among its chief instruments, and adroit managers can
channel its passion toward administrative ends. People who sing
"Solidarity Forever" are ripe for recruitment into solidarity with
overall organizational objectives, if managers appeal skillfully to
their collectivist impulses. In a case in my study, a professor
dismissed ostensibly for sexual harassment ran to the faculty
association protesting his innocence and begging for help. The
official studied the documentation, pronounced the accusations
"credible," and sat on his hands. Dr. PITA went into arbitration
without the association's support and entirely at his own expense.
He was in the end exonerated and his dismissal overturned, but
by declining to support his case, the faculty association had in
effect sided with the administrators who wanted to get rid of him.

If the first three stages of the process have been managed well and if a climate of unit-think is in place, other internal bodies to which Dr. PITA may appeal will respond along the lines described earlier for ethics tibunals. The Waterloo structure includes an internal grievance committee, its members jointly appointed by the presidents of the university and the faculty association. All the Waterloo pitas in my study approached the grievance committee for redress, but only one of them thereby secured a significant lessening of punishment. Three cases were ruled outside the committee's jurisdiction, three ended in equivocations that allowed the administrative decision to stand, one resulted in a decision in favour of the administration, and in my case the committee quit.

At the provost's and my hearing last August before the Outside Judge, I offered an explanation of why the committee in my case quit. I said it was because even though I was grieving a decision of my department chair, the committee had been informed that the deans of arts and graduate studies, an associate dean, an associate provost, the provost, the editor of the campus newspaper, as well as various professors and a prominent feminist lawyer, would all be testifying in support of the chair. Further, the university had placed its law firm at the chair's disposal. This meant that a bewildered committee of two mathematicians and a geographer found itself between an aggrieved professor on one side, and on the other side the university's entire administrative hierarchy and its legal counsel. The committee's thunder had already been stolen by the ethics tribunal, which had publicized its finding of my guilt, and by the provost, who had denounced me in the campus newspaper. Given the circumstances, so I said to the Outside Judge, the course of least resistance for the grievance committee was to find procedural excuses to quit.

In response to my explanation in the hearing last August, the provost repeated the committee's procedural excuses, but he added an important insight. It must be expected in grievance cases, he said, no matter who they are nominally filed against, that the respondent is in effect the whole administrative hierarchy. This is the key point. Any house tribunal—whether mandated to deal with harassment, grievances, employment equity, research ethics, or whatever else—derives its authority from senior management. Its members depend on senior management for career advancement. Hence once the latter has let it be known that a professor is undesirable and deserves dismissal or humiliation, a house tribunal is unlikely to thwart the elimination process—at least not if the cultural infrastructure of unit-think is in place.

Ideally, if the tribunal has been appropriately staffed, it will hear any case Dr. PITA may bring to it and return a verdict that reinforces his pariah status. In my case, after the grievance committee quit, the university president called the three members into his office and urged them to resume the hearings. A month later the committee gave its final judgment:

> We write to report on our efforts, regrettably unsuccessful, to establish rules for the resumption of hearings of the grievances brought by Professor Westhues against his department chair, and to inform you that the Committee hereby closes its investigation of this case.

This was obviously not the optimal outcome from an administrative point of view. Academic managers embroiled in pita cases often have to be content with acquiescent tribunal decisions, as opposed to confirmatory ones. Usually, the farther away from Dr. PITA's home academic unit a decision-making body is, the less likely it is to give the elimination decision outright endorsement.

Acquiescence is sometimes enough. Once the Stage-Three punishments have been imposed on Dr. PITA, he is a "marked" professor. You, as an administrator, have time on your side. The longer Dr. PITA can be left spinning his wheels in domestic tribunals, the sooner he will run out of gas. To cite my own case once more: the grievance committee quit for the first time on July 21 and for the second time on September 6, but then announced that it was writing a report explaining why it quit. This took until November 25. In the meanwhile I had to begin my fall-term classes wearing the stigma of public disgrace and waiting for a committee's report on why it would not hear my case for removing it. The stress of facing students that September was a memorable lesson in the strategic effectiveness, from a managerial viewpoint, of dragging out as long as possible the handling of Dr. PITA's internal appeals in the fourth stage of the elimination process.

24

Appeals to the board

The key managerial principle for dealing with Dr. PITA's appeals beyond the campus is this: what you cannot control, resist. To manage means to control. This is what you and your fellow administrators do for your university. It is a corporation, a person in law. You collectively are its head. Upon you falls the burden of keeping it alive and functioning. Eliminating undesirables is part of that burden, and toward that end you coordinate the body's constituent parts as best you can.

What is outside the corporate body is by definition outside your control. You need the larger world, since it supplies students and hires graduates, awards grants and celebrates results, but it is uncertain, menacing, and inclined to interfere. Especially if you are president, you can expect outsiders to try to pressure you into restoring Dr. PITA to respectability. They may write to you in aggressive and hostile tones. A judge may order you in the name of the state to do what you know will damage the university. In the face of these pressures, you guard your university's autonomy—or to use the current phrase, you "protect the integrity of the institution." This reflects the key principle: what you cannot control, resist.

By law, ultimate authority over the university lies with its governing board, and you may be surprised to see me treat it here as an external force. It must never be treated that way publicly.

Indeed, never say out loud what my pledge to give useful advice compels me to say in the next paragraph. As an administrator, you must show the same deference to the board, especially to the chair or chancellor, as ministers of the British government show to the royal family, especially to the monarch.

Despite its supreme legal status, you must never mistake the board for the head of the corporate body. The administration is the head. The board is a hat on the head, physically on top, symbolically in the superior position, but important mainly for protecting the head from other outside elements. If the head cannot sustain the weight of the hat, it will hardly have strength enough to control the body. Only the head knows what is going on. The hat on the head does not.

That senior management does and must run things is borne out by more than half a century of research on large organizations, beginning with Berle and Means's 1933 classic, *The Modern Corporation and Private Property*. Their thesis is confirmed by my own experience as a member of various boards, and for two years the board chair for a highly successful private school. Having a career of my own and able to devote no more than a few days a month to the school, I was in no position to make policy. I did what board members customarily do: reviewed the treasurer's and CAO's reports, took comfort in the CAO's assurance that things were going well, tried occasionally to say something helpful, and held my breath hoping no crisis would arise beyond what management could handle.

The implication here for the process of eliminating an undesirable is that the president should act skillfully to keep the university's governing board out of it. Most boards have a *modus vivendi* with management that defines a large arena of managerial discretion and restricts board involvement to policy issues requiring sizable expenditures. If Dr. PITA should come to the board's attention, the board should be respectfully reminded that this is a routine personnel matter that management will handle on its own. This position will be easier to sustain if the agenda for board meetings is sufficiently filled with presentations by scholarship recipients, proposals for campus beautification, and plans for the post-convocation banquet.

In three of the cases I have reviewed, two of them in small institutions, the president made the mistake of allowing the governing board to get involved. In one case, he actually asked the board to appoint an outside investigator to judge Dr. PITA's case. The board ended up awarding PITA substantial damages and the president lost face. In the second case, after allowing Dr. PITA's claims a full airing by the board, the president wisely left for a position elsewhere. The third case was Fabrikant's.

Contrast these cases with one where a pita-proxy for whom PITA's vindication had become a personal crusade undertook to provide each of the 40 members of the governing board with 100 pages of documentation about the university's trampling on PITA's rights. He ran off copies, prepared the 40 manila envelopes, and carried them in a large box to the board secretary, a week before the board's quarterly meeting. The secretary assured him the materials would be transferred. Then after the meeting had taken place, she returned the large box to him by campus mail, the 40 manila envelopes intact, with a note explaining that the board's executive committee had met beforehand, reviewed his submission, and decided this matter would not be appropriate on the board's agenda. The president in this case got his way, Dr. PITA's exclusion was achieved, and the pita-proxy took early retirement.

The all-important principle remains: what you cannot control, resist.

25

October 25, 1997

This Saturday afternoon, Waterloo held its fall convocation for conferral of degrees. I didn't go. Convocations are not my thing, though years ago I once fixed lunch on convocation day for doctoral graduands who had done their work with me.

Among the degree recipients today was a bright, high-spirited woman whose M.A. thesis I supervised back in 1992. She went on to her Ph.D., but by then I had been suspended from teaching at the graduate level. She wrote her thesis under the supervision of one of the eleven colleagues who had signed the petitions to oust me.

Some weeks ago she phoned to invite me to join her and her family for lunch today at the University Club after the graduation ceremony. I accepted with pleasure. Only later did it dawn on me that the Club would be filled today with the campus dignitaries and their guests, the worthies getting honourary degrees and awards.

In crisp autumn sunshine I joined the crowd walking up the hill to the Club, feeling like Meryl Streep in *Out of Africa* or Martin Luther at a Vatican Eucharist. To my relief, the table for my former student and her guests was in a room apart from the larger crowd.

I enjoyed the occasion. Her husband is a grade-eight teacher in the North who hunts ducks, grouse and ptarmigan. Her

126

parents, aunts and uncles are immigrants from the Mediterranean. Straight-talking folks, they were unbent by the higher learning. Her dad said this new doctor had always liked to read, even as a girl. He and her mother were aglow. "Now I can say I've been to university," her aged aunt declared, digging into *boeuf bourguignon*.

The graduate seated me on her right and her doctoral thesis supervisor on her left. He is an able scholar with good manners. None of the guests would have noticed estrangement between us. Truth is, none of the eleven departmental colleagues and I have had a real conversation during the past four years.

I had not been home ten minutes this afternoon when the fax phone rang. It was the Outside Judge's reply, addressed to the provost and me, to the fax I sent him last Monday, inquiring as to the status of his report. (Taxpayers please note how many days a week this guy works.)

"Greetings Gentlemen: Believe it or not, I haven't forgotten you in the blur of the last month. I will be back on this matter tomorrow and will let you know later next week where things stand although (obviously after all this time) I expect I will be sending the decision and reasons at that point. Regards and renewed apologies to you both."

Then my son and I went outside and raked leaves.

Suppose you run a wallpapering business, and you make a deal with a homeowner to do a job. On June 11, you give it to her in writing that the paper will be up "not later than August 1." You don't get around to measuring until August 7, but you tell her then the job will be done in three weeks. On September 2, you give her a finish date of September 9. On September 25, you say you will be done by October 3. Now if, on October 25, you fax her the note the Outside Judge faxed me today, and if she then tells you to go to hell and hires someone else for the job, do you conclude there is something wrong with her?

Fair dealing means something radically different in the world of a large university than in the world of small business. This Outside Judge I am subject to at least feels mild compunction for having broken his word four times. I suspect that makes him unusual.

I had to begin this book when I did to give myself an honest reason for not wanting the Outside Judge's report to arrive. A reason big enough to outweigh my honest yearning to know what the report will say.

Nothing but this book was reason enough. There is nothing to salvage from these past four years, if not understanding of this amazing social upheaval I have witnessed in others' lives and mine. Without this book, it is all a waste of time—and of students' tuition fees. Could this book make it a blessing?

This is an exhausting way to work. This book is born of the tension between a big reason and a big yearning grating against one another inside of me. I would not wish ever to write a book this way again.

Friends and relatives telephone, send notes and e-mails: "Have you gotten that report yet?" For anyone subjected to the politics of workplace exclusion, such expressions of concern are a lifeline. So was the invitation to lunch today. So, too, the bannock and hard tack my mate brought home to our son and me from her trip to the prairies last week. A former student's note that came Friday quoted E. M. Forster: "Only connect." Good advice. Whoever is turned into an island, dies. Whoever prevents that, redeems the world.

26

Letters from PITA's friends

Professors differ from most employees in belonging to professions and disciplines that in decades past held academic managers almost in vassalage. Presidents and deans trembled if leading lights in some field found fault with their decisions.

Today, au courant administrators realize that the influence of academic luminaries is on the wane, while large corporations, governmental funding agencies, and the mass media are in ascendancy. What makes a university's image is less and less the fame of faculty, and more and more the fit between the institution's degree programs and the new global economy. This is one reason administrative skill is more essential than formerly.

It is also a reason why today's academic managers need not shudder when dozens of pita-proxies elsewhere write letters in support of Dr. PITA. These outsiders are not part of your campus community. They do not partake of its special character. All they know is that a friend of theirs is in trouble. They are self-important enough to think you might be swayed by the arguments they set forth.

In three quarters of the pita cases I have reviewed, outside colleagues and former students mobilized in her defense. They were sometimes joined by faculty associations elsewhere and nonacademic friends. I have read about 200 letters sent on behalf of a dozen different pitas.

On account of common themes and a similar tone, these letters can almost be said to constitute a distinct literary genre. They are more passionate than obituaries, more aggressive than letters of reference. The paragraphs below are forewarning of ten typical points such letters make, lest you be caught off guard and be tempted to write an equally passionate, aggressive reply.

Apologies for intrusion. The writer is conscious of making a gratuitous intervention, and hopes admitting this will make it less unwelcome:

> Please don't take these lines as any kind of interference on my part into an affair which in terms of the legal and organizational conventions of your university system is beyond my competence.

Flattery. The letter's recipient can expect to be described as intelligent, reasonable, mature, youthful, compassionate, dispassionate, and possessed of a sense of perspective:

> I am relieved that it devolves upon you to consider the many facets of this unique situation. If there must be a Solomon, I cannot think of a more fortuitous choice than yourself as president of the university.

Testimonials to PITA's scholarship. The largest part of the letter ordinarily dwells on the excellence of PITA's research and writing, its impact on the profession, and its contribution to worthy causes ranging from remediation of environmental ills to social justice to world peace. The testimonials will strike you as overblown:

> Not only did he give birth to a branch of knowledge which now supports the intellectual effort of literally thousands of individuals, but also he has nurtured the development of this field, largely through his influence on the research efforts of graduate students at your university. It is no overstatement to say that it would be a travesty to see such a brilliant career end in the manner now proposed.

Testimonials to PITA's teaching. A former student may emphasize that PITA not only sparkles in the classroom, but cares so much that she devotes hours to students outside of class, and shapes their thinking indelibly:

Dr. PITA showed great patience answering my questions, on at least one occasion spending approximately one hour with me. I still recall this eight and a half years later, and must credit Dr. PITA for helping me to understand the subject.

Pleas for due process. A writer may be so steeped in the culture of individual rights as to call the procedures followed in PITA's case unfair, and to insist that she be given more opportunities to defend herself:

It seems unlikely that the principles of due process and natural justice have been well served in this instance. These principles are vital in the administration of justice in the case of the most humble and ordinary members of our society. In this case, I am sure I have no need to remind you that the individual involved is a highly distinguished scholar of international repute.

Impugning of motives. The ostensible reasons for your administration's action against Dr. PITA are often disputed or held up to ridicule as opportunistic excuses to humiliate him and destroy his career. The university is alleged to be "using a stupid incident to kick him out":

What has occurred is the act of a cowardly administration, afraid to submit its true reasons for terminating Dr. PITA's appointment to the scrutiny required under the dismissal policy.

Sagacious discourse. Space prevents my quoting an example here, but it is not uncommon for a writer to spend pages analysing why Dr. PITA is in trouble—always in such a way as to shift the blame away from him. The analysis may dwell on group dynamics in the academic unit, conflicting theoretical or methodological orientations in the discipline, an alleged decline in the quality of academic life, or basic aspects of human nature. Both classic and contemporary authors may be cited. The letter may appear to have taken at least a full day's work. It may have a tone of seriousness unusual in academic writing.

Threats of damage to the university's reputation. The single most common theme is that your institution's good name will be tarnished on account of its treatment of Dr. PITA, that the professional community will not look upon your university with favour unless the decision against her is reversed. Sometimes, as if to frighten you, the reputational damage is reported as a *fait accompli*:

> I write simply to express my disgust at the way the university is conducting itself in its conflict with Dr. PITA, and to report the concomitant decline in my regard for it.

Acknowledgement that PITA is not a team-player. An administrator can take comfort in the recognition some writers give to Dr. PITA's annoying eccentricity. Adjectives like *singular, difficult, prickly,* or *special* may be applied to him parenthetically. The quote below is unusually direct:

> From a bureaucratic point of view Dr. PITA may not be the easiest person to handle; he may rather appear to be a bird of paradise in the world of academics. The splendor of these birds delights us all, and it is also this radiance that has brought world-wide fame to your university in Dr. PITA's field. Aren't academic institutions those who should attempt to preserve the living space of these rare birds?

Cutting of personal ties. Most outsiders can do nothing but plead with you, but some have personal ties they can cut. Eliminating their own connections to your university is a way of identifying with the eliminated professor. One writer resigned his adjunct professorship, another sent back an honourary degree conferred years earlier, several said they would not recommend the institution to prospective graduate students, and some alumni served notice "that we do not intend now or in the future to contribute to your university."

A letter written by one president to another noted that formal rules can prevent an administrator from showing sympathy toward faculty and staff in pain: "I recognize that your hands are tied in expressing any personal concern for Dr. PITA, much as you might like to do so." This was well said. You know that in a different time and place, Dr. PITA might be counted an asset on the faculty. Your burden is to live in the here and now, to be a leader in a setting where Dr. PITA is, for better or worse, *persona non grata*. The majority of letters in my study went unanswered. The minority received perfunctory replies.

As a final means of easing any discomfort you may feel at ignoring letters sent from outside on PITA's behalf, I should tell you that at least some of the writers find an ethic of tolerance easier to champion on your campus than on theirs. Professors who cropped up as PITA's outsider-friends in some cases in my study, appeared again as his enemies, in cases in their own academic homes. It is much as in the witch-hunting era, when people often disagreed, as it was said, on which was witch. Two of the cases in my study are from the same academic unit: a professor who helped eliminate Dr. PITA became Dr. PITA three years later, and was himself eliminated.

27

Judges

Academic freedom has two legal meanings. The meaning you value for administrative purposes is *institutional*: that the university, as a corporate body, can manage its affairs, free of interference from governments or courts. Academic freedom in the institutional sense is well entrenched in Canadian and American law.

The conception of academic freedom in Dr. PITA's mind is *individual*: that he has a contractual right to teach and do research *within* the university, free of interference from colleagues or administrators. Academic freedom in the individual sense is also entrenched in law, probably also in the policies or collective agreement at your university.

In practice, these two conceptions of academic freedom conflict. A court can enforce the second conception only by violating the first. The hearing of a claim of abridgement of individual academic freedom necessarily involves opening up the university's internal affairs for judicial scrutiny and decision, which itself abridges the institution's academic freedom.

In practice, courts give priority to the institutional conception as opposed to the individual one. Few judges want to risk entanglement in academic politics. This means in effect that if your faculty will let you get by with eliminating Dr. PITA, so will the courts.

Dr. PITA probably does not know this. To him, academic freedom is his contractual right as an individual professor. If he believes that this right has been violated, that he is being unfairly run out of his job, he may cry breach of contract and set out "to sue the pants off you." Let him try. The jist of the argument your lawyers will make is that Dr. PITA's concerns are properly addressed through the internal mechanisms of the university, which he has either failed to use or used without success, and that his action should therefore be dismissed. This argument reflects the principle cited earlier: what you cannot control, resist.

Conceivably, due process has been so flagrantly violated in Dr. PITA's case that the judge will deny a motion to dismiss. Your lawyers will have other motions to make, which PITA will have to pay his lawyer to fight. Unless PITA has personal wealth, your institution's pockets are deeper than his. At worst, you may have to pay him money in an out-of-court settlement. That a court would actually order Dr. PITA's return to the faculty or the lifting of a stigma placed on him is a prospect too remote to dwell upon.

There is an exception to the normal reluctance of courts to intervene in academic matters. It is the condition of moral panic: revulsion against pacifists during the world wars, anticommunism in the 1950s in the United States, and now the biopolitical turmoil over race and sex. If Dr. PITA is female, nonwhite, or in another of the categories of designated oppressed groups, and if she can make a case of abuse, harassment, or discrimination on such a basis, a court may be more willing to intrude itself in your university's internal affairs than it would otherwise be. There is a flip side to the coin: if Dr. PITA is a white, able-bodied, heterosexual male, and if you can somehow tar him with accusations or innuendo of abuse, harassment, or discrimination, his chance of attracting a judge's sympathy is even lower than it would be otherwise.

Collectively, the undesirable professors in my study have paid lawyers more than $.5 million for advice and representation, but none of them has yet won a significant victory in court. If Dr. PITA files a court action against you or your university, you should turn the matter over to an aggressive law firm, refrain from public comment, and let the lawyers drag things out however long it takes, while you turn your attention elsewhere.

An actual case of appeal to the courts may assuage your fears of this manoeuvre. This pita did not hold a faculty appointment, instead a specialized staff position that involved regular collaboration with faculty. He had been in the job for more than two decades. The professors he assisted generally gave him rave reviews. This was part of the problem. As is not uncommon, applause from co-workers without administrative authority led PITA to think he was doing a good job, and to ignore warnings from his administrative superior that he was not.

His troubles began, so he alleged in his statement of claim, in year x, when his supervisor began cohabiting with one of PITA's co-workers. Thereafter, Mr. PITA could do nothing right. In year x+2, the supervisor rewrote his job description and began sending him letters of reprimand. In year x+4, the supervisor suspended PITA for three days without pay, and again in x+5, the reason being poor job performance. In year x+6, PITA was fired.

According to Mr. PITA, he had done his best to follow his supervisor's directives, but they made no sense. Other managers and computer experts had advised him that the directives were not doable. Mr. PITA claimed the supervisor did not understand the service he was providing to professors, and never sought out their views on whether his work was good or not. After he was fired, 22 of these professors wrote letters attesting to PITA's commitment and expertise.

Perhaps anticipating this mobilization of professors in Mr. PITA's defense, the supervisor fortified the bomb of dismissal with a further charge: sexual harassment. A higher-level manager had already conducted an investigation, interviewed four female complainants (including the woman in the relationship with the supervisor), and managers still higher on the totem pole. Thus, when Mr. PITA was informed of his dismissal, a finding of sexual misconduct was already in place, on top of the negative assessment of his job performance.

Mr. PITA crumbled at news of his firing. He went into a depression, was unable to sleep, had stomach pains, and vomited what he ate. Nonetheless, he launched an appeal, and a six-person domestic tribunal was appointed to hear it. A senior manager, the supervisor of the one who had investigated the harassment charges, sat in to advise the tribunal on university policy.

The hearing was postponed once on account of Mr. PITA's illness. The second time it proceeded, though Mr. PITA got sick part way through and was represented by the professor serving as his colleague-advisor. PITA chalked up the accusations against him to "extreme hostility." He complained about the vagueness of charges like "violating a business relationship." At the same time, he confessed to having asked a female professor for a kiss some 15 years earlier, and to having once tapped his hand on the knee of a woman sitting next to him as they drove together to a meeting out of town. This was not a sexual advance, he said, but a way of emphasizing some point he was making in their conversation. The woman had not protested at the time, he observed, but had made the return trip with him. Still, he apologized if the gesture was misconstrued, saying he was "deeply sorry" for any discomfort he had caused.

PITA's written summary to the tribunal highlighted themes recurrent in almost all the cases in my study:

> I have reflected hard on this nightmare. Am I so socially gauche as to cause people such extreme discomfort? What is wrong with me? There is one thing I can say for certain: I

have tried to be careful not to do anything to make people uncomfortable around me. Despite the care I have taken in this matter, I have been victimized by the people spreading these rumours. Surely this vicious rumour mill throws into doubt not only the testimony about alleged sexual impropriety but also testimony fabricated to depict me in the workplace as nothing more than an idiot.

The tribunal held against Mr. PITA on all counts. It acknowledged that he and his supervisor defined his job differently, but gave weight to the formal job description and the series of disciplinary letters. As for the charges of sexual misconduct,

> the tribunal has concluded that Mr. PITA engaged in behaviour which he reasonably ought to have known would have a sexual overtone and objectionable [sic] to female staff members. Also, the tribunal is prepared to believe the essential facts put forward by/about A and B; clearly, his behaviour had an impact on them.

The university president upheld the tribunal's decision, saying he could find no evidence of procedural error.

A month later, Mr. PITA sued the university for wrongful dismissal, seeking two years pay plus $100,000 in punitive and exemplary damages. For the next ten months, the university's lawyers fought to keep the case out of court. Their chief argument, in a motion for summary dismissal, was that it had already been fairly adjudicated by the domestic tribunal.

Mr. PITA fought back (his personal resources exceeded what one might have guessed). The professor who represented him at the hearing filed an affidavit that cast doubt on whether due process had been observed. The professor claimed that he had been prevented from cross-examining witnesses, that his objections to procedure had been ruled out of order, that the purpose and implications of the hearing had not been made clear, and that he had continually been reminded to maintain an atmosphere of collegiality.

The judge dismissed the university's motion, so that the case could proceed to trial.

Having run out of ways to resist a judge's rare intrusion on internal university processes, senior management now faced the prospect of public exposure of the interconnected sexual and working lives of some of its managers. The media might seize upon the story as a dog does a bone. The university might be condemned for having ignored Mr. PITA's sexual transgressions for 15 or more years. Alternatively, it might be ridiculed for having gone ballistic over transgressions that did no harm or that had not occurred. Already one complainant was saying she considered the issue resolved, and did not want to pursue it further.

Senior management wisely decided to cut its losses. Mr. PITA walked away happily with an out-of-court settlement, made on condition he not disclose its terms. He was eliminated from campus just as finally as if he had left without a fight. The only difference was money.

28

Arbitrators

The shield of institutional academic freedom does not protect senior management from arbitrators. Nor can you buy your way out of being inspected by them. They are far more of a threat than judges are. An arbitrator has authority to pick through all the dirty laundry on your institution that is relevant to a given case. More ominous still, an arbitrator has authority to order Dr. PITA's reinstatement on your faculty, or to lift punishments officially imposed.

These risks to effective management exist because your university has voluntarily established a policy or entered into a collective agreement that allows its internal procedures to be opened up to an outside arbitrator's scrutiny in cases of alleged administrative violation of a professor's individual academic freedom or some other contractual right. Waterloo's policies allow external arbitration only in cases of dismissal. Most other universities allow it also for lesser grievances.

Arbitrators are usually lawyers who make their living as judges-for-hire. University administrations and faculty associations place arbitrators of their choice on an ordered list, and call upon them in that order to adjudicate disputes. Nonacademic employers and unions do the same thing. It is not unusual for the arbitrator at the top of a university's list to be booked up when called upon. The request for arbitration then goes to the next one on the list.

Obviously, the elimination of an undesirable professor could be achieved more easily if no appeal to an arbitrator were possible. Binding external arbitration constrains and complicates academic administration in all kinds of ways. Most presidents, provosts and deans try to keep it out of the structure of governance. In most Canadian institutions, they have failed until now, and must therefore resign themselves to review of eliminative decisions by quasi-judges outside admnistrative control.

Arbitrators are the wild cards in cases of professorial elimination. This is partly because they range widely in perspicuity and perspicacity. Mostly it is because of the nature of their work. They spend most of their time adjudicating nonacademic disputes, interpreting and enforcing the terms of relatively clear-cut collective agreements in business or industrial corporations or in the public service. Given the fuzziness of typical university policies, the extent of professors' autonomy at work, the complexity of evaluating professors' job performance, and the labyrinthine convolutions of academic politics, how the average arbitrator will decide a case is anybody's guess.

The key principle should be followed yet again: what you cannot control, resist. In two of the four arbitrations at Waterloo, the university's lawyers argued from the start that the arbitrator lacked jurisdiction to rule on the matter. In one of the two cases, the arbitrator was persuaded by this argument, she stepped aside, and Dr. PITA's case was never heard. If the arbitrator decides to hold a full hearing, the single best way to couch the university's case is in terms of managerial prerogatives: that the decisions with respect to Dr. PITA are within the discretion administrators are understood to have, in order to manage the corporation. If the arbitrator cannot be fended off in this way, so that the actual charges are aired and PITA's guilt or innocence is weighed, you are stuck with a proceeding you cannot control.

Still, you have the advantage. Most of the arbitrator's experience is probably in labour-management relations outside the university, where traditions of worker-control are weak and the rights of managers to tell subordinates what to do is unquestioned. Against that background, Dr. PITA will appear to the arbitrator as a privileged employee, and you as a remarkably forbearing employer. Documenting the fact that Dr. PITA did not show up at his office for months on end may be enough to win your case. Dr. PITA's claim that fieldwork required him to be in Italy will sound self-serving and arrogant.

The arbitrator is unlikely to know much about academic life, still less about your university's special character. What the arbitrator can understand is written policies and procedures. Let PITA's lawyer discredit herself pontificating about the purposes of a university and the glories of the intellectual life. If your lawyer can show a series of instructions, however stupid, that Dr. PITA failed to carry out, and a series of reprimands placed in his file on that account, the arbitrator may rule in your favour almost automatically. The arbitrator is not paid to measure your intended elimination of Dr. PITA against the ideals you voice on ceremonial occasions, but by the mundane yardstick of procedure and precedent.

You are well advised to request that the arbitration hearing be held *in camera*. Dr. PITA may ask for this himself, if there is a morals charge against him and he fears the public smearing of his name. The advantage of a closed hearing is to keep out of public view whatever of your institution's dirty laundry is aired in it.

If arbitration of Dr. PITA's case cannot be avoided, you should bear in mind the one stick you wave (never explicitly) over the arbitrator's head: the threat of dropping him or her from the approved list for your university, and of quietly passing the word to administrators elsewhere that he or she is unreliable. Your faculty association holds a similar stick. Weak as they are, these are the only sticks by which arbitrators are held accountable. Except for these sticks, arbitrators could decide cases on a whim.

Be attentive, therefore, to the attitude of your faculty association in Dr. PITA's case. If it backs him in a militant, well-organized way, underwriting all or part of his legal fees, the arbitrator takes a personal risk in ruling against Dr. PITA. The arbitrator's name may soon be mud among faculty associations far and wide. Contrariwise, if your lawyers are militant while the faculty association merely observes the proceeding in a disinterested way, the arbitrator has nothing to lose and your good will to gain by upholding your side of the dispute.

This last point underscores the importance of promoting a climate of unit-think within your university. The extent to which you have drawn the component parts of your institution into a consensus may determine whether you win or lose the case for PITA's elimination, even if the final say is in the hands of an outsider. In all four of the dismissal arbitrations at Waterloo, the faculty association remained on the sidelines. In two of them, the university won hands down. One case is still pending (arbitrators are notorious for disregarding deadlines mandated in policy). In only one of the four cases has the arbitrator ruled in Dr. PITA's favour.

Even if you lose the arbitration case, you still have cards to play. I save for the last chapter how an arbitration loss was adroitly turned into a win.

29

The media

If the process of PITA's elimination be thought as a game of cat (senior management) and mouse (PITA), the media are like human beings with brooms. They are outside your control, powerful, and dangerous. They may strike at the mouse out of fear, or at the cat out of compassion for the mouse. Some may go for the mouse, others for the cat. A sweep may miss its aim and harm the wrong side. Both cat and mouse may end up bruised. The lesson is clear: capture your mouse where the media do not see.

You may have trouble restraining yourself. A cat ordinarily takes pride in catching a mouse, and gladly puts its trophy on display. Dr. PITA's eliminators may be so consumed by hostility that they want to "expose him for what he is" as widely as possible. In their detailed analysis of a case of professorial elimination, Mary Gallant and Jay Cross treat this as the last step of the process:

> rumors circulated legitimating at the institutional level what was sanctioned at lower levels, further crippling the victim who could then be blackballed as she attempted to go elsewhere.

But blackballing is more effective if done informally through the gossip mill or, as in a handful of cases in my study, the anonymous mailing of vilifications to other universities. There is a risk of backfire in efforts to defame PITA through public media: letters in newspapers or calls to reporters to run stories on Dr. PITA's misconduct. Outsiders may be puzzled as to what the fuss is about. Cats are often disappointed that onlookers fail to share their pleasure in the dispatch of a mouse. Anyway, cat-and-mouse games do not fit the public image of a university. Many people want to believe professors are "above that sort of thing." The less said about Dr. PITA in the public press, the better.

Some undesirable professors, especially in professional and scientific fields, eagerly cooperate in keeping their troubles out of the news, even as they fight for restoration to academic respectability. They understand that professors constitute a privileged stratum of society, where salaries are relatively high and demands relatively few, and that this aristocracy has much to lose from exposure of infighting to public view. Among undesirable professors, these are perhaps the least undesirable. They themselves insist on confidentiality. A case that ended with Dr. PITA being cleared on a morals charge dragged on for years before he told even his own grown children, whom he visited every week or two. Intensely private people feel terror at the thought of being publicly disgraced.

More troublesome are whistle-blowers who believe your administration of the university is sorely lacking in some respect. A pita of this kind may seek out the media to "expose the university for what it is." Fabrikant was such a type, and half a dozen others in my study.

Do not reduce yourself to PITA's level, or elevate him to yours, by engaging him in public debate. Do not let PITA's elimination be the occasion for reporters to get started snooping around the university. Your success as an academic manager depends on your insulating your institution from outside forces it cannot control. Have your public relations office issue press releases on research projects with marketable results, distinctions won by faculty and students, convocations, new buildings, and the latest fund-raising campaign. Keep conflict out of the news.

Today's mass media are drawn to four main topics: sex, race, violence, and fraud. If Dr. PITA is a publicity hound and has a story to tell on one of these topics, it may be impossible to keep it out of the news. Probably, however, the story Dr. PITA wants to tell has to do with academic freedom, individual rights, university governance, human dignity, decline of academic standards, campus mediocrity—and above all, the alleged treachery that has led to his dismissal or humiliation. These are not stories that sell newspapers. People accustomed to toeing the line in their jobs do not feel outrage when a professor gets sacked for stepping out of line in his. Academics arguing about the powers of the university senate do not grab the attention of TV viewers who have just seen bloody bodies on the screen. Besides all this, most professors have the media savvy of toads.

If Dr. PITA does attract the attention of a reporter who then comes to you for your side of the story, the best tactic is to decline comment with regret, on account of the confidentiality of the proceeding or the fact that the case is before the courts. If you feel obliged to say something, give assurance that these concerns are not unusual, that they are being dealt with according to policy, and that you have every confidence in a fair and just outcome.

The campus press is a special case. If a climate of unit-think has been achieved, the university newspaper can be the cat's meow for confirming Dr. PITA's exclusion from legitimate company. Senior management need not infringe upon freedom of the press. If the collective will of the campus is that Dr. PITA be eliminated, articles and letters in the campus newspaper will reflect the prevailing sentiment, to the point that eventually no one will dare to write a letter of dissent. In the case described earlier where the newspaper printed the president's detailed report of PITA's misconduct, along with his picture, only one professor (from religious studies, no surprise) wrote a letter complaining that this was a pillory.

In another case, where more than half the professoriate was initially mobilized in a dismissed Dr. PITA's defense, news of the dispute in the campus newspaper followed a pattern. First there would be a bold-headlined story giving senior management's position, then the following week some letters to the editor from pita-proxies. As months passed and as senior management dug in its heels, the letters became fewer.

It is easy to forget when passions are aroused that the only important reality in Dr. PITA's case is your academic unit. Your authority is limited by its boundaries. It is from your campus, and it alone, that PITA must be eliminated. It is only the part of her identity tied to this workplace that must be destroyed. Formally, banishment should be the extent of the punishment you wish for her. If you let yourself get carried away into trying to prevent her escape to some other workplace or way of life, especially if you seek to discredit her in public media, you risk more than a libel suit. you risk your job.

As an academic manager, the only thing you have to fear is a perception on the part of other administrators, faculty, or the board of directors, that you cannot control the academic unit for which you are responsible. You must not let it be perceived as having problems. Ideally, your academic unit is known as a place where the cat always gets the mouse, but never in public view.

30

Other outsiders

I thought of including national organizations for civil liberties and professors' rights in the chapter on the media, since it is only through the media that they impact on your university. Then I decided these organizations deserve separate treatment, because the anathemas they hurl can hurt you more than one from a local newspaper columnist.

Still, the influence of these organizations tends to be overblown. The 1996 list of administrations censured by the American Association of University Professors included those at New York (since 1990), Marquette (since 1976), and Yeshiva (since 1982) Universities, along with dozens of lesser schools that appear to have survived this severest of sanctions well enough. The two schools under censure for the longest period, Grove City College since 1963 and the College of the Ozarks since 1964, both made the 1997 list in *U. S. News & World Report* of America's top regional liberal-arts colleges. Given a choice between a decade of censure by AAUP and an hour of ridicule on network TV, most academic managers would wisely choose the first.

Besides, AAUP (and its Canadian counterpart, CAUT) respect academic proprieties, move slowly, and place public anathemas on institutions only as a last resort. I am one of the handful of pita-complainants over the past ten years on whose behalf CAUT has published to its membership a full report. The process took in my case from June 1994 to November 1996. The Waterloo administration had an opportunity for quiet compromise at every step along the way. More to the point, after CAUT did in the end uphold my complaint and publish a 10,000-word report that gave the Waterloo administration a thorough dressing down, chastising the provost in particular by name, the governing board reappointed him for a second term and left him feeling secure enough to fabricate new charges against me and suspend me without pay—over renewed objections from CAUT.

The provost may have overplayed his hand in this instance—the Outside Judge has not said yet—but the general conclusion remains: no skilled administrator should be frightened of CAUT. On the basis of my own case and ten others in which the national association was to some degree involved, I suggest three things about CAUT to keep in mind if its officials contact you in response to a complaint from the Dr. PITA in your life.

First and most important, their mentality is lawyerly. They think like arbitrators, whose merits they extol. In their view, all faculty associations should be certified as labour unions. They are versed in administrative law. The actual members of the national Academic Freedom & Tenure Committee are professors elected from varied fields and serving without pay, but the committee meets only half a dozen times a year. Full-time staff lawyers guide the committee's decision-making, bring order to its deliberations, and define the broad outlines of its approach.

This implies that CAUT officials will be interested primarily in the procedural correctness of your institution's treatment of Dr. PITA. Did his side of the dispute have a chance to be heard, according to the rules of natural justice and the doctrine of administrative fairness? Have you handled his case in keeping with your policy manual? Was there due process? It is in terms of formalities observed that the officials will be most interested in hearing your case for PITA's elimination.

The substance of the case is unlikely to command their attention. Your claim that PITA teaches in his astronomy course that the moon is made of green cheese will not move them. CAUT's investigators will have little interest in the financial crunch you claim to be in. They are unlikely to look for "real" reasons beneath the ostensive ones you cite for PITA's elimination. Their concern is mainly with technique.

On account of the union mentality, CAUT much prefers disputes in which senior management is on one side and all the faculty on the other. If unit-think pervades your campus, if many of PITA's would-be eliminators are rank-and-file professors, and if your faculty association is only weakly supporting his concerns, CAUT officials will feel their hands are tied. To the extent you can portray Dr. PITA's troubles as a dispute between colleagues, you are home free. Recall the factory-worker Pita described earlier. Why didn't her union work for her? Because her chief persecutors belonged to the union.

The second thing to know about CAUT is that it has been preoccupied for the last decade with sexism, racism, homophobia, and the other issues around which today's moral panic revolves. In almost every letter or report from CAUT that I have seen, the key question is motive. If the administration can be seen, however obliquely or "systemically," to be discriminating against women, nonwhites, homosexuals, immigrants, or other oppressed peoples, CAUT comes down hard. If, on the other hand, the administration appears motivated simply by intolerance of dissent, CAUT has trouble focussing.

Compare two cases in which Dr. PITA was fired, both much publicized. The one pita was a senior tenured professor, the other a part-time sessional lecturer. The real reason for firing the first pita, so far as I can tell, was that he had founded and built a multimillion-dollar publishing company outside the auspices of the university, for his own private gain, and publicly bragged about his success. The real reason for firing the second pita, so far as I can tell, was that he had offered his services after-hours as a homosexual prostitute, for his own private gain, and publicly bragged about his success.

CAUT publicly defended the senior management in the first case, publicly blasted it in the second case. The reason is that management had carefully circled its wagons in the first case, concealed its motives, and followed something resembling due process. In the second case, management fired PITA abruptly, with no semblance of due process, and openly admitted disliking his after-hours pursuits.

The third thing to know about CAUT is that it will probably advise Dr. PITA to respect confidentiality and keep his case out of the news until CAUT itself should decide to publish a report. CAUT is like any bureaucracy: it seeks to control. Thereby it does you a favour. A loose-cannon pita poses far more risk to your management than one who buttons his lip for fear of losing CAUT's support.

Several of the pitas in my study claim the advice to keep quiet that CAUT gave them was contrary to their interests, and they regret having taken it. In my own case, CAUT chided me for the six-page exposé of events that I wrote and that a colleague sent to 100 professors elsewhere in March 1994. It said I had thereby damaged Waterloo's reputation. Then in November 1996, CAUT sent its own, far more detailed, thirty-page exposé of the same events to 30,000 professors across Canada. The lesson here for academic managers is that CAUT shares your corporatist mentality more than might initially appear. As a corporate body, it understands the destabilizing consequences of the independent expression of ideas by individuals.

CAUT (or AAUP, in the United States) is beyond the control of any university administration. So is the relevant civil liberties association, and other organizations dedicated to

individual rights, free speech, and similar values. Yet no academic
manager should treat officials from such organizations as enemies,
at least not overtly. The better advice is to show them respect,
buy them lunch, and ask them for information about themselves.
If you, as a manager, know which of their buttons to push, they
are less a threat than a challenge to your managerial expertise.

Pressure groups are like churches, each having its own
distinctive icons. So long as you recognize which icons belong to
which, and make the appropriate rituals of obeisance, you get
along with them okay. The less obvious but greater threat is the
genuine iconoclast, an individual human being with a penchant for
undressing emperors. I am thinking of one, an independent
intellectual, free-lance journalist and civil libertarian, outside any
group's control and content to live in relative poverty. Convinced
of the innocence of a man convicted of murder, she did not stop
until he was free and the criminal justice system was disgraced.
Lately she has taken on the feminist establishment, victims' rights
groups, and as always, the courts. Academic managers have more
to fear from iconoclasts than from any bureaucratized pressure
group. The best counsel is avoidance.

Stage Five: Elimination

*We do therefor hereby signify to all in general
(and to the surviving sufferers in especial)
our deep sense of and sorrow for our errors
in acting on such evidence to the
condemning of any person, and do hereby
declare that we justly fear we were sadly
deluded and mistaken, for which we are
much disquieted and distressed in our minds,
and do therefore humbly beg forgiveness, first
of God for Christ's sake for this our error,
and pray that God would not impute the
guilt of it to ourselves nor others. And we
also pray that we may be considered candidly
and aright by the living sufferers as being
then under the power of a strong and general
delusion, utterly unacquainted with and not
experienced in matters of that nature.*

From the statement of the jurors for the witch
trials in Salem, Massachusetts, made in 1697,
five years after their conviction of 150 men and
women for various forms of witchcraft.

31

Mental illness as exit door

Some undesirable professors won't give up, even after years of isolation, hassling and punishment, or even after being dropped from the payroll. What do you do then? Among the most devastating weapons in your arsenal is a managerial designation of Dr. PITA as insane. You would normally use a euphemism: mentally ill, in need of therapy or psychiatric counselling, or suffering from a personality disorder. Whatever words you use, the idea is to define her officially as beyond reason, incapable of controlling her own behaviour, and therefore a threat to her own and others' physical safety and well-being.

Labelling Dr. PITA a nut case can contribute to her elimination in at least three interrelated ways. In so far as the label is passed along on the campus grapevine, her credibility among colleagues and students will be lost. People will go out of their way to avoid meeting her or conversing with her. When they cannot help hearing her, they will not take her seriously. They may be intentionally provocative, to see if they can "get a rise" out of her or "send her round the bend." The label is thus a means of completing her ostracization.

Both indirectly through its effect on PITA's workmates, and directly through its effect on her, an official pronouncement that she needs help may be a self-fulfilling prophecy. Human beings live up to the expectations of those around them, especially

of people in authority. Whether or not she is already acting
strange, the odds that she will act strange in the future increase,
once this expectation is set down in an authoritative letter.

To the extent that Dr. PITA internalizes the label of being
mentally ill, and possibly even if she resists it, the stage is set for
her final disappearance from campus. After finding herself crying
uncontrollably, hallucinating, or otherwise "not herself," she may
voluntarily seek long-term medical leave on psychiatric grounds.
Alternatively, the label may be used as a basis for barring her
from campus, or for prohibiting her from contact with members
of the university community, by order of the university
administration or, at its request, by a court of law.

We humans live in a socially constructed world, and
mental illness is part of that. Carl Goldberg quotes his fellow
psychologist Morton Schatzman with agreement:

All that is certain about "mental illness" is that some people
assert that other people have it. ... No one has proven it to
exist as a thing, nor has anyone described its attributes with
scientific precision and reliability.

Dr. PITA may claim that *you* are crazy, or that the entire
administrative structure of the university has gone mad. The test
really is which label will stick, hers on the corporate body, or the
corporate body's on her.

In a famous novel, the collective speaks to the offender:

You would not make the act of submission which is the price
of sanity. You preferred to be a lunatic, a minority of one.
Only the disciplined mind can see reality.

The offender, protesting, muses to himself:

There was truth and there was untruth, and if you clung to
the truth even against the whole world, you were not mad.

The novel ends with the offender ceasing his offensiveness and
finding truth in the collective discipline. This is what PITA has not
learned. It is the reason she has to go.

Examples from three different universities show how this tactic can be used. In the first case, a senior tenured professor pressed her feminist, anti-authoritarian views incessantly for years, steadily isolating herself further from administrators and colleagues. Her chief weapon was letters and memos. Her command of language was exceptional. Her missives were missiles piercing the psyches of recipients. After a while, those sent to the campus newspaper went unpublished, those to academic managers went without reply. It was just PITA spouting off again. Notes to her least favourite administrators she sometimes did not sign. She figured they could tell who she was from her handwriting. She sent one a photocopy of a holy card, writing underneath: "This is God. You are not God."

The frightened administrator phoned the campus police. Three officers came to Dr. PITA's office, invited her into the windowless room across the hall, and interrogated her there. "You sent those anonymous notes, didn't you," they said. She admitted it. Then one officer walked her across campus to a high official's office for a chat with him.

The visit from the campus police tipped Dr. PITA over the edge. Describing it as a traumatic experience, she agreed to go on sick leave. But she still kept sending those accursed memos and letters—to the president, the vice-president, and deans. She complained bitterly about how she had been ill-treated in course assignments and other ways, including now the visit from the police. She wrote her department chair:

> You sow adversity and this is apparently what you want to reap. The same goes for treachery and cruelty. I'm not saying that I myself have a huge campaign in the making against you but only that I don't expect the future will treat you kindly for doing this to me.

Believing that her university was as tainted by corruption as the Arthurs Committee said Concordia was, Dr. PITA wrote:

So now I wonder who will take it upon himself to be the next Fabrikant of this university. There are plenty of unsuspecting souls who could be targeted.

This was too much for the vice-president. Citing these quotations, he wrote to her:

The fact that you are ill cannot excuse actions that threaten or defame people. Your behaviour is inappropriate and you must stop sending these materials immediately. I am concerned that there has been little improvement in your behaviour from a year ago when you were sending anonymous threatening materials. If this behaviour continues, further action will be taken which may include limiting your access to the University.

At last report, Dr. PITA was on medical leave again.

At a different university, a high-achieving young scientist paying his own soft-money salary applied for a tenure-track position. He was the ratebuster *par excellence*, employing his own research staff while at the most junior rank. He applied for a regular faculty position in four successive competitions and was turned down every time. It seemed to him that rules and procedures were being juggled to disqualify him. Being of non-European origin, he cried racism. The vice-president's appointed investigator discounted that charge, but said this Dr. PITA had been exploited by his department and penalized for good performance. The case was reminiscent of Fabrikant's.

Dr. PITA did the university a favour in the midst of his lobbying for a tenure-track job by remarking at the end of a visit with the dean, "If the competition is not going to be fair, I would rather be dead." The dean assured him the competition would be fair, then passed the word along that Dr. PITA had threatened suicide. This news gave colleagues and administrators a new lens, the lens of mental illness, through which to view Dr. PITA's subsequent manoeuvres to land a permanent job. The upshot was that when the vice-president eventually offered Dr. PITA a temporary, soft-money appointment to ease his transition to some other university, he prefaced it with a requirement that Dr. PITA undergo assessment by a qualified psychiatrist:

> You must understand that your colleagues in the community have become increasingly concerned about you. Your colleagues are alarmed by your threats of self-harm, including a hunger strike, and of the hardship you are inflicting upon yourself and your children by refusing to accept your pay cheques. They are concerned you are not behaving rationally and some are afraid for their own well-being. Whether correct or not, there is a deep and abiding concern that you may need professional help. Unfortunately, concerns for your well-being are increasing not diminishing.

Dr. PITA refused the offer. He was eventually served at his office with an eviction notice, and the campus police arrived to enforce it. Dr. PITA was also banned from the university under threat of being charged with trespassing, except that he can visit a specific place on campus at a specific time if he obtains prior police permission. That is how things stand, two years after his official elimination.

The third case shows that sometimes even academic managers get lucky. Here Dr. PITA became convinced, after 30 years of quiet, genial, productive scholarship, that unaccountable mandarins were turning his Canadian university into a mini-police state. He described the harassment tribunal as a kangaroo court:

> Ironically, these officious poohbahs who police everyone else are often guilty of inequitable, incompetent or even dishonest decisions on all aspects of university life. And people who protest such unfairness are either ignored or promptly taken care of—whether by being cowed through severe discipline or enticed into early retirement.

He said this in a magazine with half a million subscribers. He said similar things in campus media. He was also asking that senior management intervene to correct the divisions and conflicts in his department.

The vice-president offered Dr. PITA an early-retirement package and sat down with him to explain it, but Dr. PITA said no. Shaking his finger in the air, he said if he had to work four years more in the abusive conditions of his department, he would find ways to punish the administrators responsible. The vice-president took this as a threat of Fabrikant-style violence, and gasped when Dr. PITA referred to the academic managers as ten little Indians, taking this as a reference to the Agatha Christie play in which ten little Indians get murdered. He decided to suspend Dr. PITA and have him arrested for uttering threats. He also put a private investigator on Dr. PITA's tail.

Here Lady Luck entered the picture. Some weeks earlier, after vandalism at his home, Dr. PITA had purchased from a U.S. mail-order house what is commonly called a stun gun, and had it shipped to the post-office box he had rented for years across the American border. The P.I. followed Dr. PITA across the border when he picked up the stun gun and returned with it to Canada. This was two days after Dr. PITA's conversation with the vice-president.

It turns out that stun guns are illegal in Canada. When the police arrived to arrest Dr. PITA for uttering threats, they now also had a weapons charge to lay on him. An associate vice-president filed the affidavit that cooked Dr. PITA's goose. She said she and other administrators were concerned that Dr. PITA was mentally ill:

> In recent weeks, the Defendant's behaviour has become increasingly erratic and unpredictable, culminating in threats of violence against ten unidentified members of the University's administration.

The affidavit claimed the vice-president had told her that during

his meeting with Dr. PITA, the latter had said he expected the
university's board of governors

> to compensate the Defendant voluntarily for "thirty-one years
> of administrative abuse" as an alternative to a lawsuit the
> Defendant intended to file against the University.

The judge acted quickly. By the end of a day that began
with Dr. PITA going merrily across the American border to pick
up his mail, he was in jail, and served with a court order not to
possess any firearm, nor to intimidate any university employee,
nor to come closer than 250 metres to any such employee except
his wife, nor to communicate "verbally, electronically, or in
writing" with any such employee except his wife (or the vice-
president, if administratively necessary). A few months later, Dr.
PITA accepted the early-retirement package offered earlier.

Like the first two cases, this one illustrates how useful the
label of mental illness can be in the process of professorial
elimination. This is an admittedly aggressive tactic, but when a
professor starts claiming the university is a mini-police state, what
else is a manager to do?

32

November 2, 1997

Today, Sunday, my mood is heavier than five weeks ago. I wrote then that I wanted to seize an interlude in my biography, the period of waiting for the verdict of the Outside Judge. I am still waiting. These weeks have reminded me that a person's biography has no interludes. What may look like time out is just the next chapter, the next thing on the single list of things that constitute a person's life.

The weather has reminded me. I began this book in the warmth of early fall. There was still the feel of Labour Day. By now most leaves have fallen. It snowed last week. Night before last kids were out for Halloween.

My heaviness is also due to the subject matter of this book. A writer always has to choose between what is and what could be. Never have I focussed so completely on what is as during the past five weeks. Goethe wrote that whoever takes people as they are makes them less than they are. Have I made my readers less?

Do you know how naive I am? Make it a test of how naive you are. What does the term, *cat-and-mouse game*, mean? I thought it meant a cat chasing a mouse that usually gets away. The picture in my mind, maybe from cartoons or fairy tales, was of the cat waiting by the hole, the mouse peaking out, the cat falling asleep, then the mouse making its escape. Ha, ha!

Last week, before using the term in the chapter on the media, I thought I should look up its precise definition. It is a situation, so my dictionary says, where one person has another in his power, teasing and harassing him for a time before disposing of him. Then there is a quote from a newspaper, that what gave the Nazis greatest satisfaction was a cat-and-mouse game in which they would give their victims hope one day, and the next day take it away.

Funny, I have seen cats play the game. We had one years ago that enacted the game over and over in front of her kittens, for their education, only she used baby chipmunks instead of mice. She had never acted like that before she had kittens. We fed her well. Neither my wife nor my son nor I could bear the sight. That may be why I fancied a mirthful meaning for the term.

I do not want to write a book that Goethe would abhor. Carl Goldberg tells the story of a Balkan boy who cannot resist watching when his older step-brothers subject a woman to bestial rape. The watching is an evil act that paves the way for the boy years later, during the Yugoslav conflict, to join in mass murder. Am I contributing through this book to the "psychic numbing" Goldberg sees as predisposing a person to do evil?

Yet what good is it to deny empirical realities? They are what social science is about. Was it good that I pushed from my mind the sight of our cat torturing chipmunks to death? Goethe helped make Doctor Faustus a household word, but that did not make Goethe a Satanist. Surely it is not wrong for me to tell true stories of Doctor PITA in universities.

One thing is sure: platitudes will not do. The Supreme Court of Canada last week handed down its decision in the case of a 70-year-old businessman pita in Winnipeg. He had sued for wrongful dismissal in 1986, when he was fired after sixteen years with his employer. For the next eleven years, the company claimed the man was let go for just cause, the grounds being insubordination, conflict of interest, incompetence, and hindering customer relations. The company dropped this claim shortly before the Supreme Court handed down its judgment.

In a 6-3 decision, the court said the man was fired in bad faith and in an abusive, insensitive, and unfair manner. The court said

> a person's employment is an essential component of his or her sense of identity, self-worth and emotional well-being. Accordingly, any change in a person's employment status is bound to have far-reaching repercussions. The point at which the employment relationship ruptures is the time when the employee is most vulnerable, and hence most in need of protection. When termination is accompanied by acts of bad faith in the manner of the discharge, the results can be especially devastating.

The plaintiff's lawyer said everybody in Winnipeg believed the man had done something wrong, that the firing ruined his career, that he had been unable to find another job and eventually filed for personal bankruptcy. The court agreed that what had happened was wrong and that the man had suffered greatly. Even so, it denied his request for $15,000 in punitive damages. It awarded the fired employee 24 months salary. The author of a book on wrongful dismissal said it was a victory for employers, since

> it is going to take an extraordinarily abusive firing to trigger punitive damages in future cases.

33

Endings

Most attempts at professorial elimination are aborted in the first two stages. One professor rolls his eyes to another at the mention of a third colleague's name, and is met by a cold stare. A department chair tries tormenting his would-be Dr. PITA with disagreeable course assignments or some other hassling, but is stopped by the dean. Dozens of times a day in every university, somebody tests the waters to see if an elimination process can be commenced. Usually, the process dies aborning.

This book has been about cases that make it to a third stage where an incident happens or is made to, such that war on Dr. PITA is officially declared. Beyond that point, as previously chapters have explained, the institution cannot back down without suffering a degree of the same humiliation intended for the undesirable individual.

The good news for academic managers is that this outcome is rare. My survey of academic cases supports Leymann's conclusion from his Scandinavian research: in no case has a university backed off with an apology *and* readmitted Dr. PITA to full respectability.

In the majority of cases in my study, Dr. PITA made an exit through dismissal, early retirement, resignation, death, or long-term disability on physical or psychiatric grounds. My sample is too small and serendipitous to let me say so conclusively, but

I believe these are statistically the most common expressions of Stage Five. I know of two cases where transfer to a different department was proposed but did not materialize. The high degree of specialization in academic fields probably militates against transfer as a solution to the problem of Dr. PITA; it may be more common in nonacademic workplaces.

You, as an administrator, have a special interest in cases where Dr. PITA's elimination was only imperfectly achieved—that is, where the eliminators suffered a degree of humiliation and the institution substantial expense. You have still more interest in those few cases where the process failed—that is, where PITA had to be accepted back into legitimate company.

Before describing two cases of a successful but messy conclusion, and two of failure, I should underscore that all the cases in my study have succeeded to the extent of crippling Dr. PITA's career as a scholar and researcher. Whether his field was a branch of mathematics unknown to me or something more understandable like Russian history, pedagogy, epistemology or eastern religion, whether she was doing immunology or optics or botany or geology, Dr. PITA's career went on hold for years. Eliminators who carry the process through to Stages Three and Four have the satisfaction of making Dr. PITA's life unproductive and miserable for an extended period, even if his or her name is eventually cleared.

The businessman exonerated last week by the Supreme Court of Canada won two years salary—minus what his lawyer charged. Yet the company that fired him managed to keep him in official disgrace for eleven years: from 1986, when he was 59 years old, to now, when he is 70. By any reckoning, the company walked away with a fair consolation prize.

I had lunch today with a pita from another city, a prominent scholar in his field until three years ago. He continues his fight, but a final resolution is probably years away. He wanted me to hear again the story of how he was thrown to wolves by the institution that meant the world to him. I listened and offered encouragement, but I could see that no matter what happens down the road, he has already been eaten up. Recovery, if it happens, will take years.

My good fortune is to have been forced only to sip the gall that has been forcibly choked down others' throats. I know how dismissed professors feel, because I myself have come close. I can say in a public, systematic way what the professor I lunched with today cannot for lack of strength: that yes, dear administrators and professors who are bent on eliminating some colleague from your midst, you can do it. You have only to bind yourselves into a single, overpowering force, and mind the p's and q's I have described in earlier chapters. Even if you fail two or five or ten years from now, those are years of PITA's life you have taken away for keeps. Is that not in itself a victory?

One pita, the most academically distinguished in my study, spent two years off the university payroll after he was alleged to have resigned. He appealed inside and outside the university, colleagues elsewhere wrote letters, the faculty association and CAUT intervened. Papers on and off campus ran stories. Judges made rulings. So did an arbitrator. Lawyers sent their bills.

Following the case closely from the start and acting as a pita-proxy during it, I often doubted that the elimination effort would be turned back. After two years, it was. A new president took office, one who lacked his predecessor's personal investment in the cause. PITA was offered a deal: reinstatement to his tenured position at half salary until retirement, with no teaching duties. He took it. His chair, dean, and the other would-be eliminators lost face when the deal was announced, but they kept their jobs.

Six months before the deal, when his official future was still in doubt, this pita told an interviewer:

Yes, the darkest times are over. Defense has become a way
of life. ... The important success for me has spiritually
happened. The faculty association, academic people from
everywhere, and former students have spiritually made me
feel that I've won.

By now the deal has been in effect more than four years. It has
enabled PITA to have a decent life, to maintain productive
relations with colleagues elsewhere, and to give students overseas
the benefit of his teaching. Students at his home university, the
one that pays his half-salary, scarcely know he exists. He is
socially no longer part of the institution that is paying him.

The pita let go on grounds of financial exigency is the only
one in my study to have later received an official admission of
guilt and an apology from the eliminating institution. Six months
after his departure from the campus, also after the departure of
the president who was his Chief Eliminator, Dr. PITA and the
board of governors resolved their differences in an exchange of
letters published by prearrangement in the campus newspaper.

From the board chair to Dr. PITA:

I write in particular to acknowledge that the Board has not
had in place policies and procedures related to terms and
conditions of employment that have been adequate to meet
all circumstances. In its failure to have such policies and
procedures in place, the Board's dealings with you fell short
of providing you the support and processes that we believe
should be available to faculty members, both at the College
and in the wider academic community. On behalf of the
College board, I apologize to you that in these important
instances our handling of these matters was not fair to you.
I also apologize for the personal distress caused you.

From Dr. PITA to the board:

What hurt me most from 1990 to the decision in 1994 to
terminate my contract was not the College's failure to follow

adequate policies and procedures. Rather it was the "deaf ear", or dismissive attitude, of the College Board, administration, and many of my College colleagues when these failures and inadequacies were repeatedly pointed out by me, and by respected individuals and associations who spoke on my behalf. Despite the remaining mysteries, I share in the hope expressed at the close of your letter that a positive relationship can be restored.

Despite this rare exchange, this was not a case of failure of an elimination process. By the time the letters were published, Dr. PITA was on the faculty of another university, and no longer seeking official reinstatement in the campus community from which he had been expelled.

The Dr. PITA who lampooned the learning-disabilities bureaucracy and was later charged with sexual harassment appears at this writing to have turned back the eliminative effort so decisively that it must be counted a failure. He never received an apology, and the college principal continued to express confidence in the accuser's sincerity and the fairness of the harassment officers. Nonetheless, Dr. PITA obtained an official finding of not guilty from the college board and its appointed investigator. The board paid the legal expenses Dr. PITA had incurred, and awarded him a year's study leave at full salary. In this case, the mud slung at Dr. PITA obviously boomeranged.

There is finally the case of the swim coach dismissed for sexual harassment but now reinstated. The official finding as of now falls short of not guilty. It is more like a permanent stay of proceedings. Still, given that he is back on campus while the university president has taken leave on grounds of psychiatric disability, this case of intended elimination has to be considered an unmitigated disaster from a mangerial point of view. Indeed, as a result of this case, the university's acting president has lately ordered a review of the verdicts of the harassment tribunal in eleven additional cases, saying they all were procedurally flawed. This one much publicized fiasco may in the end damage the star chamber at this institution beyond repair.

What sets these two cases of failure apart from the others in my study is that the charges were too obviously contradicted by evidence. The most specific charge against the professor was that he had demeaned a female student in class by calling her "Lucky Lucy." Unfortunately, this student's cooperation had not been secured beforehand. When she learned of the complaint, she insisted she had not been demeaned, that the moniker was friendly, and that Dr. PITA was a superb teacher. In the swim coach's case, there was the problem of the e-mails and photographs.

These two cases of failure are also set apart by the targets' loud, public protestations of absolute innocence. Neither of them gave an inch: no confession of poor judgment, ill-chosen words, lack of sensitivity, or modest impropriety. Neither showed the slightest empathy for his accuser, or willingness to take her point of view.

These two cases point again to the importance of formulating charges vaguely, of emphasizing confidentiality, and above all of keeping the story out of public media, if the elimination effort is to succeed.

34

An ending to beat all

Play the cat in its worst nightmare: a bloody, bedraggled mouse, almost lifeless after prolonged tossing back and forth, suddenly springs to life and is poised for vengeance. What do you do?

This nightmare was real in a case in my study. The story begins with a tenured Dr. PITA who had worked quietly for decades in a fractured department. A private sort of man, he kept to himself. He taught his classes, told jokes to passing colleagues, ran experiments in his lab, and went home to his family. He would later be described as "a dynamic teacher who appeals, particularly, to bright students who have a thirst for learning."

Dr. PITA was foreign-born and of recognizable ethnic origin. For this reason, professional jealousy, or who knows what, there was no love lost between Dr. PITA and his department chair. Mainly, they stayed out of each other's way.

Then came the incident. Two young women who worked in Dr. PITA's lab presented themselves to the dean in a state of profound emotional upset, complaining that they had been sexually harassed. They spoke of sexual touching and prolonged kisses and hugs, to the point that Dr. PITA once said he had an erection. There were also ribald jokes, conversations about breast size, racial slurs, and overt hostility. What went on in the lab was shameful, the women said. A third accuser materialized, claiming Dr. PITA had trivialized her work and been unprofessional.

171

The chair, dean, vice-president and president all agreed that Dr. PITA had to be dismissed. He was suspended with pay pending an arbitrator's hearing of his appeal. His research money was returned to the funder. His lab was dismantled. Stories appeared in the press of an unidentified professor dismissed on a morals charge, but without details.

On account of the customary delays in scheduling, the arbitration did not commence until 16 months after Dr. PITA was suspended. All this while, and for the further 13 months until the arbitrator's decision was handed down, Dr. PITA sat at home, afraid to show his face on campus, terrified that publication of his name would bring disgrace on his wife and children. He developed health problems, though none so serious as to disable him.

The university pulled out all stops in the arbitration. The three complainants told their stories. Female colleagues testified that years earlier Dr. PITA had kissed them, or tried to, after lunch in a restaurant. Former students and lab assistants said he sometimes put his hand on somebody's shoulder or touched her arm or stood very close when discussing experiments in the lab. They said his mannerisms made them uncomfortable, though they did not at the time make formal complaints.

Dr. PITA protested his innocence. He admitted the touches but claimed they were without sexual intent. Along with the witnesses he called, many of whom reported finding his mannerisms endearing, Dr. PITA said he regularly joked and teased, trying to lighten up the atmosphere in his lab. He admitted to encouraging irreverent banter.

The dismissal policy called for the arbitrator to hand down her decision within two months of the end of the hearing. She took five months. It would be fair to say that Dr. PITA's nerves by this time were shot. Metaphorically, he was a bloody and bedraggled mouse. His only consolation was that so far, his name had been kept out of the papers. He had been relieved that the arbitrator had held the hearings *in camera*, and had promised to identify him only as Dr. X in her report. Even if he was in the end eliminated, his name might still be kept out of the papers and his family spared disgrace in the wider community.

Then, by a few strokes of her pen, the arbitrator brought him back to life. She found Dr. PITA not guilty of sexual harassment and directed that he be "reinstated to his position with full compensation, if any is owing." Of Dr. PITA's chief accuser, the arbitrator wrote:

> Whether it was because she was emotionally unstable, because she feared for her job when the second accuser came to the lab, or for some other motive need not be answered. The important finding in this proceeding is that the first accuser's allegations of sexual harassment against Dr. X are wholly unsupported by evidence.

The arbitrator dismissed the second accuser with equal finality, explaining that she had done no more than repeat the first accuser's accusations:

> Why the first accuser related to the second accuser what the adjudicator concludes were exaggerated and unfounded stories about Dr. X's alleged sexual advances for the three days the second accuser worked for Dr. X is not something that needs to be determined. What is critical is that she did, and that the second accuser believed her stories, even though she herself had observed none of the alleged sexual advances. The second accuser testified that when she heard all the stories the first accuser was telling her about Dr. X grabbing at her breasts and sexually kissing her, she became concerned for her own well-being. Accordingly, when the first and second accusers went to the dean, the second accuser spoke with conviction in reporting to the dean what turned out to be false accusations from the first accuser.

The arbitrator found the third accuser no more truthful than the first two:

Not only does the evidence of the third accuser lack credibility generally (in that it has been shown to be internally inconsistent with previous statements made by her), but also it does not square with the balance of probabilities and has not been supported by the evidence of other witnesses..., who were generally present in the lab when she was. Overall, the third accuser's evidence has demonstrated itself to be unreliable and does not support a complaint of sexual harassment against Dr. X.

Nor was the arbitrator impressed with the university's other witnesses:

This adjudication is not concerned with conduct between colleagues. To what extent a friendly kiss between colleagues may or may not be appropriate is not the issue.

The arbitrator did more than beggar the prosecution's case. She portrayed Dr. PITA as a good and decent man, dedicated to his family and his profession:

As Dr. X put it, he lives for science. He reads scientific literature voraciously and talks enthusiastically about it to whoever will listen, including, most particularly, his graduate students.

The arbitrator went so far as to quote irrelevant comments by witnesses on PITA's side, as if purposely trying to cast him in a favourable light:

This witness believed that Dr. X worshipped his wife. She observed that in all the years she has known Dr. X, he has never said one negative word about his wife.

Now suppose you were senior management in this case. What would you do when the arbitrator's report arrived in the mail? Turn tail and run? After two and half years of paying Dr. PITA to stay home, countless hours of administrative time, and

$50 or $100 thousand in legal fees, your elimination effort has collapsed. It is not just that Dr. PITA must be reinstated. Once the arbitrator's report becomes public, the chair, dean, vice-president and president will all be shown to have built their case on lies. Dr. PITA's earlier complaints about prejudice and procedural unfairness will gain credibility. The wrong heads will be on the chopping block.

You think creatively. The arbitrator has made a curious provision on the final page of her 43-page report. She applauds Dr. PITA for acknowledging now that fatherly touching is not appropriate for a professor, and she expresses her confidence that "he will not again knowingly touch his students or engage in banter in his lab that can be misinterpreted as having a sexual overtone." Still, she concludes, he should engage in follow-up counselling for one year. She does not explain why, nor say what kind of counselling it should be. Maybe she intends this provision as a sop to the feminist movement, or as a way of helping you save face. Maybe the counselling is to help Dr. PITA recover the self-confidence you have robbed him of. Remember, I told you arbitrators are wild cards.

Quickly, before Dr. PITA has time to say or do anything more than feel relief, you issue a press release:

An adjudicator has overruled the university's decision to dismiss a faculty member charged with sexual harassment, concluding instead that the individual be reinstated and undergo counselling.

In the adjudicator's view, the conduct was not of such a serious nature as to render the faculty member clearly unfit to hold a tenured appointment, and therefore she ordered that the faculty member be reinstated.

The president expressed support for the women students and staff who brought the faculty member's inappropriate behavior to the attention of the university, and stated that the university remains committed to the provision of a harassment-free study and work environment.

Consistent with the wishes of the individuals involved, the university will not be making the adjudicator's report public.

The media pick up the story. There is public outrage that a guilty professor got off with a slap on the wrist. One headline reads, "Dirty Professor Reinstated." Another quotes the vice-president's explanation for why the report would not be released:

We are in a tricky position in that we have been ordered to reinstate this faculty member, and so anything that could be seen as compromising our ability to do that successfully would be a real problem.

If this Dr. PITA had been of a different temperament, he might have identified himself, released the report, and sued the university for libel. In fact he was tired, overjoyed at being exonerated, and understandably fearful that he would never live down being publicly linked to a morals charge. He accepted the university's offer of an early-retirement package, and signed a statement agreeing to keep the terms secret. Having won his 30-month fight for reinstatement, he resigned.

It cost something, but the cat still got its mouse.

35

November 12, 1997

Since finishing the "ending to beat all" a week ago, I have been writing footnotes, correcting mistakes, seeking colleagues' comments on the manuscript, and catching up on chores postponed during the six weeks of writing. I finally cleaned the leaves out of the eavestroughs yesterday—good thing, too, since it snowed overnight.

This morning, Wednesday, frustration with the Outside Judge got the best of me again, and I faxed him a further inquiry:

> It is outside my experience that a senior official of a major university, entrusted by the president of a sister institution with a matter of consequence and urgency, and requested by him to provide a decision in a month and a half, would still not have provided the decision after five months. Three times now—on 2 September, 25 September, and 25 October—you have faxed the provost and me a friendly note leading us to expect your report "next week," but the report does not arrive.

> On 25 October, you wrote that you would let us know "later next week where things stand although (obviously after all this time) I expect I will be sending the decision and reasons at that point." But I heard nothing from you the next week, nor the week after that. Please give us an update at your earliest convenience.

An hour after I sent the fax, the Outside Judge faxed back his reply:

Forgive me for misleading you. "The road to hell is paved with good intentions" was a favourite saying of my mother's, so I ought to know better, but this exercise is outside my experience as well. The president's entirely reasonable request is nonetheless one at which I would have balked had I known the volume of materials that would be provided to me. However, the greater incursion on my ability to finish has been the inability to find any stretch of time, i.e., more than a couple of hours.

Precisely because the matter *is* of consequence, I cannot issue my decision until I have the opportunity to review and check it in its entirety. But I do owe you both an apology for not communicating as I indicated I would, and I realize I will have to make time.

I *will* send the decision by courier one week from today. Thanks for your patience. Kind regards.

Notice that the Judge agreed this matter is of consequence. Not just for me. There are consequences also for the Judge: his career depends on who he makes his friend, and who his enemy. The gravest consequences are for the University of Waterloo. Once an institution has officially dragged one of its members through mud, any mud wiped off by outside authority dirties the institution.

I predict this Outside Judge will try to wash as much mud as possible directly down the drain. I saw no mean streak in him, and he does not share our local passions. He seemed an old-fashioned professor who likes to talk things through. At the same time, he is loyal to the managerial fraternity—note the respect his note shows for the president who got him into this mess. I predict the Judge will look for ways to blame policies, and to keep individuals clean. Can he launder all of us?

36

November 20, 1997

"The hardest thing to do is to tell what is going on," Arthur Miller said in 1956. "It's easy to talk about the past and the future, but nobody knows what is happening now." Through drama, Miller did the hardest thing. I have tried to do it here in a nonfiction way: to tell what is happening now in the governance of universities.

If the Outside Judge had kept his word, he would have sent his report by courier yesterday, and I would have received it today. When it had not arrived by eleven-thirty this morning, I telephoned his secretary. She professed to know nothing about it, but would phone me back.

An hour later, while I was on the phone checking e-mail, the Outside Judge himself left me a long voice-mail.

"I had hoped I would get in touch with you today before you had to call me, and I apologize that that wasn't the case. I'm still proofing the decision, and in fact I'm still finishing the portion on the policy itself. Obviously, from my last missive, I really did think I would be able to send it yesterday."

He explained how a family medical emergency had kept him at a hospital last weekend, and that he leaves this afternoon for an all-day meeting tomorrow at another university. He apologized again, and said he didn't want to make personal excuses.

"I don't know whether I'll be able to send the document tomorrow, but if you can give me your home address, I should be able to send it by Saturday, so that you will have it on the weekend.

"You will not be disappointed, I don't believe, with the decision. I think you know that I had concerns about it from the beginning, and I have upheld your appeal. The reasons, frankly, have to be carefully done, and they are detailed. I don't want to send it until I'm absolutely sure that I have it right from my perspective, and I'll just ask you, if you can, to exercise some more patience."

I phoned back and left a message with his secretary thanking him for the update and suggesting, in case he might have forgotten, that he should give the same information to the provost. I gave his secretary the provost's telephone number. I asked her to tell her boss that if I seem hypersensitive to procedural matters, he can understand why.

I'm glad to be informed that the decision is in my favour. Part of me wonders what stock I should put in the Outside Judge's spoken word on the report's substance when he has broken his written word six times on its date of delivery. The larger part of me is confident.

Academic administrators range on a continuum between those who behave as bureaucrats in their relations with faculty, staff and students, and those who respond as whole human beings. The former come across as efficient, neutral, disinterested managers, concealing or repressing the passions that nonetheless underlie what they do. I have never gotten along well with them. I never know where, if anywhere, they stand, except higher in the pecking order. They don't like to be teased. Dissent is insubordination.

From our first meeting last summer, the Outside Judge struck me as located toward the continuum's opposite end:

committed to his administrative role, but first of all a person. He has continued to impress me so even while misleading me about when his decision will arrive. He *answered* my queries about its lateness. He said he was sorry and made the kind of excuses human beings make. By responding as he did, he reduced himself to my level, as one fly caught in the web of history trying to come to terms with another fly. He has never behaved as if he were not of my species. He doesn't act like a spider. Or God.

Still, the decision is not real until it is received on paper by the president, provost, and me. Until then, the official findings of guilt hang around my neck, as they have for four years. That is a long time, but nowhere close to a record. Besides, I am still alive and kicking.

Word has come that one undesirable in my study, after twice as many years fighting stigma in vain, has had a heart attack. In another case, the news is that Dr. PITA's spouse almost died last week of a ruptured ulcer. I'm sure that in the course of being eliminated, some undesirables find themselves divorced or separated from their husbands or wives. This has happened in only one case in my study, and then only temporarily. In the rest, Dr. PITA's wife stood by him. Her husband held firm. A supportive spouse is among the strongest shields protecting an undesirable. You can never completely humiliate a person who is loved at home.

37

November 28, 1997

Instead of waiting at home last Sunday, hoping a courier would bring the report from the Outside Judge, I might as well have gone Christmas shopping with my mate and our son. Nor did Monday bring the news I have been led to expect over and over since this book began.

On Tuesday morning I hit the road for Missouri, to spend the American Thanksgiving with my mother and other relatives. Normally I am teaching on the U.S. holiday, since the Canadian Thanksgiving comes earlier, on the first Monday in October. My sabbatical this fall has allowed me to join my family of origin's harvest festival for the first time in 20 years.

Yesterday, the holiday evening, fortified with turkey, yams, pumpkin, good talk and Boonslick wine, I got news from my mate of another fax from the Outside Judge. It came yesterday morning, she said, handwritten on stationery from a Toronto hotel. She read it to me over the telephone:

Gentlemen: Thanks for your continuing patience. I will be reviewing the final draft of my decision when I return home this weekend. I will confirm its status with you on Monday.

Academic antics are a long way from where I am tonight: my mother's antebellum cottage on Third Street in Glasgow, a rivertown well off the interstate, home to just 1,295 souls. In Ontario, almost that many undergraduates are sometimes packed

182

for class into a single lecture hall, where individuality cannot matter. Here, in this less rational scatter of homes, churches and businesses spread across the bluffs, the human variety can show. People can be themselves—or come closer to being so. Decades ago, my eyes fastened on the World, I looked down on my hometown. No longer.

Mom and I drove down to Main Street this evening, to watch Glasgow's Christmas parade. The two blocks were darkened on this windless night, the better to show off the strands of lights strung from one end to the other on both sides of the street, and the hundreds of candle-lanterns lining the sidewalks. These latter had been made by cutting the tops off translucent milk jugs—a shovel of sand in the bottom of each one weights it and holds the candle upright. Standing beside the car with Mom, chatting with cousins and former schoolmates, and feeling the unseasonable warmth and moistness of the air, I found the scene more moving than any Christmas display I have yet seen.

Maybe 300 people were on hand to watch the parade. They stood in clusters among the parked cars, and spoke in hushed voices. Hand-holding teenagers strolled about. Without fanfare, there emerged from the darkness at the street's far end the silhouette that headed the parade: Joseph in a flowing robe leading the donkey on which Mary rode, modestly wrapped in a long blue shawl. The crowd was so quiet you could hear the animal's hooves on the pavement. Then came 50 schoolkids under a banner that said something about Jesus's birthday. There were two floats on the back of trucks, a beauty queen in a convertible, and two horse-drawn wagons, one with the mayor and the other with Santa Claus. The parade was all of three minutes long.

Later, transported into cyberspace, I learned of a debate at the Outside Judge's university between him and a sociology professor. He, as one of the three-man team administering that institution, has published in the campus newspaper an essay opposing faculty unionization:

> Aren't the attributes of the right kind of university and
> professorial unity, collegiality and accountability to be found
> at the negotiating table (or in the decision of an external
> arbitrator) rather than on the picket line?

We should be making common cause, he says, engaging in real
conversation, and working together.

In response, the sociology professor says roughly what I
said eighteen months ago in Waterloo's campus newspaper, after
the provost and president here published a similar rallying cry
against unionization. My sociologist-colleague says the Outside
Judge is part of an "imperial administration prone to issue
ukases," pretending to listen to faculty but behaving as if "it and
it alone knows what needs to be done." My colleague also reports
the Outside Judge's salary: $178,000, almost double the big bucks
I make. Should I take it as a compliment that my case is in the
hands of one of the highest-paid professors in Ontario?

If we learned doctors were serious about making common
cause, and escaping the moral and financial costs of internecine
war, we would sit down at the feet of the uncredentialled men
and women who brought off the Christmas celebration Mom and
I watched tonight. These small-town folks have just raised $31,000
to repair the town's historic library after damage from a fire, and
they pooled their tractor-power earlier this fall to build a new
track for their high school's award-winning team.

The town is economically depressed. Megastores an hour's
drive away have killed business after business on Main Street. The
local factory pays wages near the legal minimum. Corporate
agriculture has put the squeeze on family farms. To get an annual
income of $178,000, you would have to stand eight or ten workers
shoulder to shoulder.

Somehow, despite hard times and abundant differences,
these people seem to get a lot done together. I am sure they

would be willing to show and tell us how they do it. They value and respect universities, supporting Missouri's public ones with tax payments and private ones with tuition cheques. In these ways they are already making common cause with us. They read books, too: one woman came over to our car tonight to tell Mom how much she had enjoyed her autobiography. Another complimented me on my books. And if those country folk are now as they were when I was growing up, by and large they keep their word.

38

December 5, 1997

I arrived home last Sunday night, ready to receive on Monday the Outside Judge's promised confirmation of the status of his report. No communication from him arrived.

On Tuesday morning, I faxed him:

I acknowledge with thanks your fax of 12 November, your telephone call of 20 November, and your fax from Toronto of 27 November. The last of these indicated that you would confirm to the provost and me on Monday the status of your decision. Since I did not hear from you yesterday, I am writing to inquire if your decision has been sent, or if it is further delayed.

On Tuesday evening, I found two almost identical one-page faxes sent in reply that afternoon from the Outside Judge's office. It was the fax I had just sent him, except that the bottom half of the page, everything after my "Sincerely yours," was blank. It looked to me that he had handwritten his reply on the bottom of my inquiry and tried to send it back to me, but that on account of a malfunction in his machine, the bottom half of the page had failed to transmit. I therefore faxed him back a note asking him please to try again.

He did so on Wednesday morning, and this time the reply he had written on Tuesday came through:

Gentlemen: Sorry, I was in a meeting until 10:30 last night

and had left you both a handwritten note with my secretary but I neglected to leave the fax numbers. I'm still dithering over some of the wording and can't get clear to spend any time on it until tomorrow afternoon. I'll confirm by the end of the week the delivery of the decision and reasons. Thanks for your patience.

Now it is Friday night. I suppose it is appropriate that he has not confirmed "the delivery of his decision," since no delivery has in fact occurred. My only news of the Outside Judge is two further letters published this week in his university's campus newspaper, lambasting his polemic against faculty unionization.

Dithering! My dictionary says the word means "to waver with uncertainty or fear." Were I in the position of the Outside Judge, I cannot imagine telling the parties to the case that I am dithering. The fellow deserves high marks for honesty. Were it not for this book and its destination in the larger world, the one beyond Ontario universities, I would have spent this entire autumn spinning my wheels in the rut of the Outside Judge's dithering.

Thank God for the larger world. It is the only refuge for people burned by their employers. If they cannot psychologically remove themselves from the workplaces that humiliate and stigmatize them, they are toast. I got a sermon to this effect this week from one of the pitas whose cases form the basis of this book. She was preaching to herself as much as to me. It's about time I took her advice.

39

December 10, 1997

Reading these final, admittedly repetitive updates is an appropriate concluding way of letting the reality of the eliminative process sink in. Gentle reader, do you feel as if hung out to dry? Still, all books must end. Today, Wednesday, the Outside Judge has ended this one.

He missed his deadline of being back in touch by the end of last week, but on Monday night he faxed the provost and me a further handwritten note:

Gentlemen: Please forgive my continuing inability to give you a reliable delivery date. I have been putting in vile hours (Saturday and Sunday as well) and the demands of my regular duties haven't yielded any time since I last wrote. I'll correspond again later in the week. (Unfortunately my assistant is on bereavement leave until the new year, so I'm scrambling to compensate.)

If the formal efforts to usher me out of this university had not been underway already for four years, I might have more of the trust and patience the Outside Judge has asked of me. As it is, both these quantities are in short supply. I faxed back this reply last night:

Thank you for your faxes of 2 and 8 December. I am sorry for the stress in your life, not least because it has exacerbated the stress in mine: the disheartening experience of being misled nine times (list attached) about when to expect your report, the repeated need to defer other decisions that depend on yours, and the unexpected prolongation of what Justice William Brennan called the "wrenching disruption of everyday life" that being charged, investigated, and judged constitutes even for a defendant who is in the end acquitted. At the same time, I have appreciated your giving us progress reports and assurance of your thorough and detailed consideration of this matter, I am pleased to know that you have upheld my appeal and that the decision is finished except for "dithering over some of the wording," and I know there are many claims on your time. I look forward to hearing from you further as you indicate.

Just after midnight last night, the fax phone rang. Both my wife and I were asleep. By the time I awoke, she had hit the alarm clock, leapt out of bed, and gone in to awaken our son for school. Then the phone stopped ringing, my wife came back to bed, and I lay awake wondering what fax might have come in.

I got up and went downstairs to see. There was nothing. Then I remembered that I had left the upstairs fax machine, the one that seldom works, plugged in. At that same moment the fax phone started ringing again and I frantically pushed buttons trying to get the downstairs machine to answer. It would not. Its screen kept saying "Sleep," which is what I eventually went back to. This morning at the university, I read the fax the Outside Judge had tried to send to our home last night:

Dear Professor Westhues:

Just before leaving my office, almost exactly fifteen hours after arriving there this morning, I pulled your letter off the office fax machine. You are right. In my concern to be responsive to your repeated requests to know when my written decision would be forthcoming, I have been unduly optimistic and I apologize for misleading you.

I do think, however, that it is time I clarified a few things:

1. As the president and I have never met or even conversed (my name was given to him by another), his June 11th request that I provide a written decision by August 1, 1997, was just that—a request.

2. I travelled to Waterloo three times: once to meet with you when the provost was on vacation, once to meet with the provost when you were on vacation, and once to hold the hearing on the first available date thereafter—August 7th. By that point it was abundantly clear that the president's request could not be met.

3. I am not sure that the president would have requested a written decision by August 1, 1997, had he known that your submissions to me (which he also requested that you be permitted to make) would include over 1100 pages of closely printed text.

4. Nevertheless, at the conclusion of the hearing on August 7th, I said the following:

    > I was supposed to be on vacation starting Monday for three weeks. But I'm going to spend part of the time doing this so I don't want to think that you will have to wait until September. I expect you won't. I'll get this done as soon as I can. (transcript, p. 36)

5. I did not, in fact, get even one week's vacation during the summer and I have had no significant stretches of time free since.

I therefore propose not to write to you again until I have the decision in hand. Sincerely yours.

Let me conclude this book with the reply to the Outside Judge I faxed to him and the provost half an hour ago:

I acknowledge with thanks your fax of 9 December. Considering that it was written at midnight after a 15-hour workday, I think your reply shows admirable restraint. I'll look forward to receiving your report when it is done. In the event that this is not until the new year, I should take this opportunity to wish both you and the provost respite from administrative pressures over the holidays, and a joyful Christmas season. Sincerely yours.

40

December 11, 1997

I know I told you yesterday that it was the end of the book, but another fax came this afternoon, a copy for me of a note from the provost to the Outside Judge:

I am sorry to add to your pile of paper, but I do need clarification on one point. In his December 9th letter to you, Professor Westhues states, "I am pleased to know that you have upheld my appeal." Have I missed something? The messages I have seen indicated only that you were still working on your decision. Sincerely yours.

I do not know today when or if any further word from the Outside Judge will arrive. My thoughts now necessarily turn to the three courses I am scheduled to teach next term. Whatever else lies in store, this sabbatical will end on January 1.

If I had a functioning crystal ball, I would know that the next word I get from the Outside Judge will be seven weeks from now. At 6:30 AM on Monday, February 1, 1998, a fax will arrive, a copy for me of a letter from the Outside Judge to the president:

I expect to send you my decision, with copies to Dr. Westhues and to the Provost, by courier on February 10, 1998.

The last word goes to a friend of mine outside the academy, a man no one would guess is an expert on the elimination process: "Ken, don't you know? It never ends."

Notes

Foreword

For discussion of Leymann's research, see Ch. 15. The ILO study is described in "Violence on the Job: a Global Problem," a press release of 20 July 1998, published on the web-site at www.ilo.org

Goldhagen's book is entitled *Hitler's Willing Executioners* (New York: Random House, 1996).

The articles cited at the end are: Howard S. Becker, "Whose Side Are We On?" *Social Problems* 14 (1967), pp. 239-47; and Alvin W. Gouldner, "The Sociologist as Partisan: Sociology and the Welfare State," *The American Sociologist* 3 (1968), pp. 103-116. The quote at the end is from *Leviticus* 19.

1. Carpe diem

For review and interpretation of the disciplinary actions against me in 1993-94, see John Fekete, *Moral Panic: Biopolitics Rising* (Montreal: Robert Davies, 1994), pp. 267-286; and Roman Dubinski, "CAUT to Report on Westhues Grievance," *FAUW Forum* (October 1995), pp. 2-6. For a different take on the same events, and developments in 1995, see Roger Gannon, Patrick Grassick, Glenna Knutson, Patrick O'Neill and Gail Storr, *Report of the AF&T Committee into the Complaint of Professor Ken Westhues*, insert to the *CAUT Bulletin* (November 1996), 8 pp. Published with this report are responses to it by James Downey, Ronald Lambert, Adie Nelson, and me. Beginning in June 1994, first without consulting me and then over my objections, the Waterloo administration made available on the internet a number of relevant documents at http://www.adm.uwaterloo.ca. These include Sally Gunz, Don Brodie, and Patti Haygarth, *Report of the Ethics Hearing Committee* (May 9, 1994); Jim Kalbfleisch, "Open Letter to the University of Waterloo Community" (June 6, 1994); Ronald Lambert, "The Westhues Case: a Statement of Fact" (October 1996); commentaries on Lambert's document by Jeffrey Shallit and Roman Dubinski;

a letter from Gail Paton Grant of March 24, 1994; and two letters of mine (March 15 and June 2, 1994) to colleagues at other universities. Later, I asked that my letter in the *UW Gazette* of March 15, 1996, be added. As of January 1998, nobody has released documents from the second ethics proceeding (1996) or the discipline imposed on me by the provost in 1997. The publication that prompted the latter is a booklet I published myself in 1996 for classroom use, *The Risks of Personal Injury in Liberal Education: a Warning to Students*; I sold 1,000 copies that year, but have not yet sought a commercial publisher for it.

Methodologically, this study is rooted in pragmatist and humanist traditions of scholarship, traceable to Alexis de Toqueville, William James, Jane Addams, and the early Chicago school of sociology, and represented more recently by C. Wright Mills (*The Sociological Imagination*, New York, Oxford, 1959), David Riesman *et al.* (*The Lonely Crowd*, New Haven, Yale University, 1950) and Robert N. Bellah *et al.* (*Habits of the Heart*, Berkeley, University of California, 1985). I have sketched these traditions in my introduction to and selections for *Basic Principles for Social Science in Our Time* (Waterloo, Ont.: St. Jerome's University, 1987). The procedure followed for the present study was to immerse myself over the past several years in the roughly two dozen cases. When I sat down to write on September 28, I surrounded myself literally with the stacks and file-folders of documentation on these cases, as well as two working papers on this topic that I wrote in 1994 and 1996. I wrote the names of all the undesirable professors on a single sheet of paper, and kept this in front of me as I sat at the word processor, weighing my depiction of the general process point by point against the individual cases.

The quotation from James is from his 1906 lecture, "What Makes a Life Significant?" in J. L. Blau, ed., *William James: Pragmatism and Other Essays* (New York: Pocket Books, 1963), p. 273.

2. Readership
The quotation is from John Kenneth Galbraith, *The Age of Uncertainty* (Boston: Houghton Mifflin, 1977), p. 60.

Here and throughout, I draw on Max Weber's portrayal of recent Western history as a process of rationalization; see H. H. Gerth and C. W. Mills, eds., *From Max Weber: Essays in Sociology* (New York: Oxford, 1946).

3. The problem of Dr. PITA
Anybody who writes about cases of professorial elimination faces the question of whether to identify parties by name. The answer depends on the purpose of the article or book.

If the purpose is to hold individuals accountable for their actions or to correct injustices, the writer usually names everyone involved. John Fekete, in *op. cit.*, appropriately identified the main players in the 17 cases he wished to bring to public attention.

Disclosure is sometimes prohibited by law. In preface to her exploration of events surrounding expulsion of a college master at the University of Melbourne (*The First Stone*, New York, Free Press, 1997, p. 235), Helen Garner notes that Australian law forbids identification of complainants in cases of alleged sexual assault. Generally, so does Canadian and American law. University policies often allow confidentiality to both sides in cases of alleged unethical behaviour.

Libel chill discourages giving names. Garner reports that her publisher's lawyers went so far as to insist she not only refrain from naming one charcter but disguise her as several different characters.

What law and policy allow, kindness or literary grace may yet forbid. Fekete did not name students. Garner reports:

Soon, however, more and more people I had interviewed asked not to be identified. Now everyone in the text bears an invented name.

The question of whether to name people has an easier answer in a book like this, whose purpose is not to argue the merits of any case but to abstract from many cases a general pattern. Such a purpose makes names irrelevant. Mary Gallant and Jay Cross give nobody's name in their article on essentially the same process I analyze in this book: "Wayward Puritans in the Ivory Tower: Collective Aspects of Gender Discrimination in Academia," *Sociological Quarterly* 34 (1993), pp. 237-56.

Being proud of the parts they have played in the campus dramas that form the basis of this study, some administrators and professors may be disappointed not to find their names in these endnotes. Most will feel relief. These dramas vary in how much publicity they have received, the range being from lots to none. To avoid the awkwardness of naming some people but not others, and to keep the reader's mind focussed on the general pattern, I decided not to name anyone. Full citation is provided to writings (like Garner's book or Gallant and Cross's article) that have helped me make sense of the data, but not to writings that constitute the data (letters, memos, newspaper articles, reports).

The author's case is an exception. As Thad Snow says in *From Missouri* (Boston: Houghton Mifflin, 1954, p. 7), "I may express judgments and reveal bias, and the reader has the right to know how to appraise them." Hence the references to previously published accounts in the endnote to the first chapter. Some are friendly toward me, others hostile. Responsibility for what they say rests with their respective authors and publishers.

5. Marks of undesirability

The quotation is from W. I. and D. S. Thomas, *The Child in America* (New York: Knopf, 1928), p. 572.

8. Millennial fears

Mary Jo Deegan tells the story of Thomas's dismissal on pp. 178-186 of her *Jane Addams and the Men of the Chicago School, 1892-1918* (New Brunswick, NJ: Transaction, 1988).

The flavour of anticommunist fear in the U.S.A. a few decades ago can be tasted in transcripts from hearings of the House Committee on Un-American Activities. See Eric Bentley's edited collection of transcripts: *Thirty Years of Treason* (New York: Viking, 1971).

The quotation from Thad Snow is from *op. cit*, p. 266.

Christopher Lasch made his critique of the "survival mentality" in *The Minimal Self* (New York: Norton, 1984), No less relevant to the current cultural climate is Lasch's last book, *The Revolt of the Elites and the Betrayal of Democracy* (New York: Norton, 1995).

On contemporary preoccupations and anxieties surrounding violence, especially sexual predation, see Fekete, *op. cit.*; Charles J. Sykes, *A Nation of Victims: the Decay of the American Character* (New York: St. Martin's, 1992), especially Chapter 3, "The Roots of Victimism"; Wendy Kaminer, *It's All the Rage: Crime and Culture* (Reading, MA: Addison-Wesley, 1995); and Donna Laframboise, *The Princess at the Window* (Toronto: Penguin, 1996). Fekete and Laframboise both make methodological criticisms of the research of the Canadian Panel on Violence against Women. They accuse its report (*Changing the Landscape*, Ottawa, Ministry of Supply and Services Canada, 1993) of exaggeration and fear-mongering. Accuracy aside, the report remains a cultural artifact that testifies to the prevailing mood.

10. Which lesson from Fabrikant?

My account of the Fabrikant case is based on four sources: Paul Kaihla, "Concordia's Trials," *Macleans* (Nov. 9, 1992); Harry W. Arthurs, Roger A. Blais, and Jon Thompson, *Integrity in Scholarship* (Montreal: Concordia University, 1994); John Scott Cowan, *Lessons from the Fabrikant File* (Montreal: Concordia University, 1994); and Morris Wolfe, "Dr. Fabrikant's Solution," *Saturday Night* (July/August 1994). My reason for identifying the undesirable professor in this case is the exceptional horror of its conclusion, which has shaped the consciousness of academic administrators across Canada and beyond.

11. Deep trouble

The classic article cited here is Harold Garfinkel's "Conditions of Successful Degradation Ceremonies," *American Journal of Sociology* 61 (1956), pp. 420-424. Other relevant sources from symbolic interactionist sociology include Edwin M. Lemert, "Paranoia and the Dynamics of Exclusion," *Sociometry* 25 (1962), pp. 2-25, reprinted in his *Human Deviance, Social Problems, and Social Control* (Englewood Cliffs, NJ: Prentice-Hall, 1967); Howard S. Becker, *Outsiders* (New York: Free Press, 1963); and Erving Goffman, *Stigma: Notes on the Management of Spoiled Identity* (New York: Free Press, 1963).

The Milton quote is from *Paradise Lost*, Book I.

12. Sanctions

The quotation from William Miller's book, *Humiliation and Other Essays on Honor, Social Discomfort, and Violence* (Ithaca, NY: Cornell University, 1993) is on p. 157. Of no less relevance here is Avishai Margalit's *The Decent Society* (Cambridge, MA: Harvard University, 1996). Margalit's definition of a decent society is one "whose institutions do not humiliate people" (p. 1), defining humiliation "as the rejection of a person from the human commonwealth and as the loss of basic control" (p. 3).

13. The small matter of truth

The reference is to Daniel A. Farber and Suzanna Sherry, *Beyond All Reason: the Radical Assault on Truth in American Law* (New York: Oxford, 1997). In his review in *The New Republic* (October 13, 1997, pp. 40-43), Richard Posner faults the authors for playing the "Jewish victim card" against the people-of-color victim card. To the extent a political and judicial issue becomes a question of who has been victimized the most, truth does not speak to power, but vice versa.

I rely on Plato's account of Socrates's trial in the *Apology*. See B. Jowett, tr., *Plato: Apology, Crito, Phaedo, Symposium, Republic* (Roslyn, NY: Walter J. Black, 1942, 1969).

Burdened by the legacy of the Enlightenment, university administrations have been reluctant to claim the right to define for their faculty what is true and false. The bolder among them may take lessons from ecclesiastical administrations. Harvey Cox's *The Silencing of Leonardo Boff* (Oak Park, IL: Meyer-Stone, 1988) is a readable and up-to-date exposition of the Roman Catholic case. Professorial elimination in the university is generically similar to what is called *disfellowshipping* in one of the more successful American religions; see Heather and Gary Botting, *The Orwellian World of Jehovah's Witnesses* (Toronto: University of Toronto, 1984). Daryl and Kendall White describe the disciplining of Mormon intellectuals in "Charisma, Structure, and Contested Authority: the Social Construction of Authenticity in Mormonism," *Religion and the Social Order* 6 (1996), pp. 93-112. On the other hand, ecclesiastical arbiters of truth are too outdated to serve as models. Orwell (*Nineteen Eighty-Four*, London, Penguin, 1954, 1989, p. 214) described the new oligarchies as "less avaricious, less tempted by luxury, hungrier for pure power, and, above all, more conscious of what they were doing and more intent on crushing opposition." If Orwell is right, the present book can be understood as an instrument of consciousness-raising.

14. October 11, 1997
See M. D. Frankfurter and G. Jackson, eds., *The Letters of Sacco and Vanzetti* (New York: Penguin, 1997). On the advisory committee's role, see pp. 358ff of Appendix I, Felix Frankfurter's story of the case.

15. Leading Leymann's mob
Leymann's summary article is "Mobbing and Psychological Terror at Workplaces," *Violence and Victims* 5 (1990), pp. 119-126.

John Ralston Saul's book, *The Unconcscious Civilization* (Toronto: Anansi, 1995), is based on his Massey Lectures at the University of Toronto. The quotation here is from p. 34f. Saul's estimation of the corporatist trend may reflect the fact that he is an independent intellectual, not on the payroll of any thinktank or university. Academic managers can take comfort in knowing that his is a dying breed: see Russell Jacoby, *The Last Intellectuals: American Culture in the Age of Academe* (New York: Basic Books, 1987).

16. Necessary harm
Fergal Keane's book is entitled *Season of Blood: a Rwandan Journey* (London: Penguin, 1996). The quotation here is from p. 173.

17. The star chamber
On the proliferation of tribunals and the growth of administrative law, see Gerald L. Gall, *The Canadian Legal System* (Toronto: Carswell, 1990), especially Chapter 12, "Fairness and Natural Justice in the Administrative Process." On the meaning of due process, see Walter K. Olson, *The Litigation Explosion* (New York: Penguin, 1992), especially Ch. 13, "Naked to Mine Enemies."

On the mentality out of which harassment tribunals have been created, an especially illuminating reference is the Chilly Collective, *Breaking Anonymity:*

---

the Chilly Climate for Women Faculty (Waterloo, Ont.: Wilfrid Laurier University Press, 1995). The chapter by Lella MadhavaRau, the former Race Relations Officer at the University of Western Ontario, describes the travails of her office.

Having found no single book that subjects the Star Chamber to thorough examination, I have pieced together this account from partial treatments in encyclopedias and books on English legal history.

18. Making the star chamber work

The value of ethics tribunals as an administrative resource first became clear to me from Heinz Klatt's paper, "A Sexual Harassment Policy as a Tool of Power and a Weapon to Censor, Harass, and Control," a revision of which appears in *Sexuality and Culture* (Volume 1, 1997), pp. 45-70. See also his "Regulating 'Harassment' in Ontario," *Academic Questions* (summer 1995), pp. 48-58.

With respect to Point 10, the question of bias or prejudice against the respondent in a proceeding, the most congenial precedent is from the Sacco-Vanzetti case. After their sentencing, according to Felix Frankfurter (*loc. cit.*, p. 359), influential citizens submitted to the governor evidence of prejudice against the defendants on the part of Webster Thayer, the judge who had made the key rulings against them. The question of Judge Thayer's impartiality was referred to Judge Thayer himself, who found that he had been without prejudice.

The reference to the police officer in Point 17 is from an address by Harry G. Black, Q.C., "The Disciplinary Process: Parts V and VI of the Police Services Act," given to a conference of the Police Association of Ontario on August 21, 1996.

19. Managing moral panic

On the deceptiveness of academic appearances with respect to moral panic, Hermann Melville's characterization of Billy Budd's Chief Eliminator is apt: "Though the man's even temper and discreet bearing would seem to intimate a mind peculiarly subject to the law of reason, not the less in heart he would seem to riot in complete exemption from that law, having apparently little to do with reason further than to employ it as an ambidexter implement for effecting the irrational" (Chicago: University of Chicago, 1962, ch. 11; first published 1924).

The quotation from Fergal Keane, *op. cit.*, is on p. 173.

The quotation from Thad Snow, *op. cit.*, is on pp. 260, 267.

The quotation from Harry Truman is from Merle Miller's "oral biography," *Plain Speaking* (New York: Berkley, 1973), p. 447.

The quotation from Nathaniel Hawthorne, *House of Seven Gables* (Ch. 20), is as given on p. 79 of John M. Taylor, *The Witchcraft Delusion: the Story of the Witchcraft Persecutions in Seventeenth-Century New England* (New York: Gramercy, 1995).

The quotation from Anne Llewellyn Barstow, *Witchcraze: a New History of European Witch Hunts* (New York: HarperCollins, 1994), is on p. 39.

So far as I know, the classic sociological work on the phenomenon of moral panic is Stanley K. Cohen's *Folk Devils and Moral Panics* (London: MacGibbon & Kee, 1972). Gustave Le Bon's *The Crowd* (New York: Viking, 1960, first published 1895) is another classic source. Insightful recent contributions to the general theory include Erich Goode and Nachman Ben-Yehuda, *Moral Panic: the Social Construction of Deviance* (Oxford: Blackwell, 1994), and Arnold Hunt, "'Moral panic' and moral language in the media," *British Journal of Sociology* 48 (December 1997), pp. 629-48.

The literature on the curent panic surrounding race and sex on university campuses is by now voluminous. The discussion in this book is informed by the following sources: Fekete, *op. cit.*; Garner, *op. cit.*; Laframboise, *op. cit.*; M. Patricia Marchak, *Racism, Sexism, and the University* (Montreal: McGill-Queens, 1996); Gretchen von Loewe, *Forgotten Promise: Race and Gender Wars on a Small College Campus* (New York: Knopf, 1996); Christina Hoff Sommers, *Who Stole Feminism? How Women Have Betrayed Women* (New York: Simon & Schuster, 1994); Daphne Patai and Noretta Koertge, *Professing Feminism: Catuonary Tales from from the Strange World of Women's Studies* (New York: Basic, 1994); Warren Farrell, *The Myth of Male Power* (New York: Berkley Books, 1993); Shelby Steele, *The Content of Our Character* (New York: Harper, 1991); Kate Filion, *Lip Service* (Toronto: HarperCollins, 1996); Neil Bissoondath, *Selling Illusions: the Cult of Multiculturalism in Canada* (Toronto: Penguin, 1994); Jean Bethke Eshtain, *Democracy on Trial* (New York: Basic, 1995); Peter C. Emberley, *Zero Tolerance* (Toronto: Penguin, 1996); Jonathan Rauch, *Kindly Inquisitors* (Chicago: University of Chicago, 1993); Jane Gallop, *Feminist Accused of Sexual Harassment* (Atlanta: Duke University Press, 1997); Robert Hughes, *Culture of Complaint* (New York: Warner Books, 1993); Katie Roiphe, *The Morning After: Sex, Fear, and Feminism* (Boston: Little, Brown, 1993). The discussion here reflects also my reading of the now defunct *Balance*, a magazine published at the University of Alberta, the Toronto-based *Newsletter* of the Society for Academic Freedom and Scholarship, *Academic Questions* (the journal of the National Association of Scholars in the United States), and ongoing coverage in *The Globe and Mail* and Southam newspapers, of human tragedies that the current panic has left in its wake. Articles and columns by Sandra Martin, Richard Gwyn, Donna Laframboise, Margaret Wente, Robert Fulford, and Robert Matas have struck me as exceptionally astute.

20. October 19, 1997

George Soros's article was entitled "The Capitalist Threat," *Atlantic Monthly* (February 1997).

My 1985 lecture from which the quotation is drawn was entitled "Becoming Rootless by Degrees"; abridged versions were published in the *UW Gazette* (November 27, 1985) and *Past and Present* (December 1985). Most of my later entries into campus debate over policy-making and governance appeared between 1990 and 1993 in *FAUW Forum*, a monthly publication of Waterloo's faculty association that I helped found in 1988. I have the impression that the main articles that touched a nerve were "The Faculty of n.e.c." (December 1990), "Alan George Bows Out" (April 1992), and "In Defense of Explanation and Apology" (January 1993), as well as a letter in the *UW Gazette*, "Women in sociology: a note about the past" (November 22, 1989).

21. No playful romp

The metaphor of a city on a hill is from *Matthew* 5:14. John Winthrop (1588-1649), governor of Massachusetts Bay Colony, applied it to the Puritan society he ruled. Nicholas Hytner, who directed the film version of Arthur Miller's *The Crucible* (New York: Penguin, 1996), recalled the metaphor, "an image of perfection," to make sense of the Salem trials: "The constant pressure to dedicate every aspect of life to the glory of God is what lets the devil in..." ("Filming the Crucible," p. xvi). From medieval Christendom to Puritan Massachusetts to Stalinist Russia to postwar America, high hills are associated with deep swamps.

For the quotation from Chesterton I am grateful to Donald T. DeMarco of St. Jerome's University.

Photographs of the members of Reserve Police Battalion 101 and of the targets of their eliminationist fury are reproduced in Christopher R. Browning, *Ordinary Men* (New York: HarperCollins, 1992) and in Daniel Jonah Goldhagen, *op. cit.*

22. Unit-think

This chapter is based on Irving L. Janis, *Groupthink* (Boston: Houghton Mifflin, second edition, 1982), especially Ch. 8. The quotations are from pp. 11 and 13.

24. Appeals to the board

The full citation is A. Berle and G. Means, *The Modern Corporation and Private Property* (New York: Macmillan, 1933). Christopher Lasch (*Revolt of the Elites,* pp. 52f) discussed the conundrum of producing knowledge that, if disseminated, might destabilize the social order.

25. October 25, 1997
The quotation from E. M. Forster is from *Howards End*, Ch. 22.

27. Judges
The distinction between institutional and individual conceptions of academic freedom is from Michael P. McDonald, "A Lawyer's Brief against Litigating Academic Disputes," *Academic Questions* (fall 1992), pp. 9-18. Bernice Schrank, former chair of the AF&T Committee of CAUT, has argued that Canadian courts have defended the individual conception very weakly. See her "Academic Freedom, Speech Codes, and the Search for Truth," *McMaster University Faculty Association Newsletter* (April 1994), pp. 14-17. She offers a capsule description of Dr. PITA, a quote from John Dos Passos on Thorstein Veblen: "Veblen asked too many questions, suffered from a constitutional inability to say yes."

29. The media
The quotation from Gallant and Cross, *loc. cit.*, is on p. 239.

31. Mental illness as exit door
The lines from Morton Schatzman are as quoted in Carl Goldberg, *Speaking with the Devil* (New York: Penguin, 1996), p. 148.
     The quotations from Orwell's novel, *op. cit.*, are pp. 261, 226.

32. November 2, 1997
The line from J. W. von Goethe (*Wilhelm Meisters Lehrjahre* 8.4) is as quoted by Werner Stark in *The Social Bond, Vol. IV: An Investigation into the Bases of Law-abidingness* (New York: Fordham University, 1983), p. 128. Let me acknowledge here my debt to Stark, who fathered me intellectually during my first years of teaching.
     The Balkan boy's story is in Goldberg, *op. cit.*, Ch. 9, "The Forging of the Malevolent Personality."
     The account of the Supreme Court decision is from Kirk Makin, "Insensitive firings not tolerated," *The Globe & Mail* (October 31, 1997).

36. November 20, 1997
The quotation from Miller is as given in Bentley, *op. cit.*, p. 824.

37. November 28, 1997

A Kansas City magazine has published an engaging account of the track-building project in Glasgow. See Jim Tucker, "Community Puts Cooperative Spirit on Track," *Farmland System News* (November 1997).

39. December 10, 1997

The quotation from former U.S. Supreme Court Justice William Brennan is as given in Olson, *op. cit.*, p. 278.

Afterword

A book is one moment in a conversation. I want to say thanks to those whose ideas this book reflects and responds to. I want to say please to its readers.

First the *thanks*. Besides those named in the chapters and notes, about 200 colleagues, students and friends have shaped this book by sharing with me their insights on the subject matter. I am grateful to all the participants in the case studies, eliminators and eliminated alike, who entrusted information and opinion to me. A dozen of those who tried to make helpful public comments on my own case found themselves on the firing line: disparaged in the press, denounced over the Internet, shunned in academic gatherings, and otherwise punished. I regret the cost to them of their help to me, and wish it were possible to thank all these individuals publicly by name without fear of upping that cost.

An anecdote can underscore my gratitude. A colleague from across campus—I could place him as a professor though we had not met—was using the photocopier. I stood a respectful distance back, waiting my turn.

Noticing me, he observed, "I was thinking of you the other day." He paused to change the page.

My stomach tightened. It was a time, I had reason to believe, when the thoughts most colleagues were thinking about me were not thoughts I cared to be reminded of.

"Yeah," he went on, flashing a friendly grin. "I came across a woodcut of Spinoza during his darkest days. It showed him walking down the street with his nose in a book, with everybody else shrinking away as if he had a contagious disease."

What generosity! Here were spontaneous kind words, and at the same time independent support for an idea that would eventually find expression in this book: the essential sameness of Dr. PITA in his or her varied manifestations.

Hundreds of similar communications have influenced how this book turned out. I am grateful for each of them.

I cannot exclude from appreciation even the hostile communications, of which there have been quite a few. However much insight this book holds into the elimination process, whether much or little, there would be less without data from my own experience. I wrote in 1994:

> I have high regard for every single one of the participants in the mob action against me. History is full of examples of good and decent people being caught up in fanatic movements that do a great deal of harm. As an undergraduate in a church college 30 years ago, I myself took part in a kind of witch hunt that caused great and undeserved pain to the professors who were vilified.

Now the *please*. I want to encourage readers as strongly as I can to contribute in their respective ways to our further understanding of the elimination process. This book does not pretend to be the last word on anything. It is an invitation to action, and to study, reflection, and research.

Many questions beg for detailed, systematic answers. How does workplace elimination affect the spouse and family of the one eliminated, and what part in the process do they typically play? Could one empirically identify six or eight or ten distinct types of undesirable? Which psychological attributes distinguish eliminators from undesirables, and to what extent is the difference situational? The biggest question is how to explain variation in elimination rates. Why do some families, groups, organizations, and societies need to eliminate undesirables regularly and *en masse*, while others seem to get along productively while building almost everybody in?

All such questions depend on recognizing and getting a feel for the process itself. Toward this end, I heartily recommend reading relevant dramatic and literary works. Dostoevsky's Grand Inquisitor is alive in our time. So is Mrs. Hutchinson, the woman who gets the marked paper in Shirley Jackson's short story, "The Lottery." A friend has been insisting that I see or read Friedrich Dürenmatt's play, "The Visit." I intend to.

Among the technological marvels of recent years is the availability at low cost of enriching, entertaining motion pictures in video rental stores. I list below two dozen of those currently stocked that dramatize various aspects of the elimination process. Viewing these films, and others like them, brings home the centrality of elimination to human affairs and raises questions that social science has barely begun to answer.

A Man for All Seasons (Columbia, Fred Zinnemann, 1966). Paul Scofield stars as Thomas More, England's former lord chancellor, beheaded for treason in 1535. More went from favoured to undesirable in the space of six years, for resisting the centralization of power under Henry VIII.

The Crucible (Twentieth Century Fox, Nicholas Hytner, 1996). Here Paul Scofield plays Judge John Danforth, Chief Eliminator of the witches at Salem. Explaining why he cast Scofield in the role, Hytner wrote:

> It would have been easy enough to find one of those actors who specialize in the sinister, but Danforth's particular danger is that his convictions are genuine and his commitment to rooting out the Devil is deeply felt. (*op. cit.*, p. xxv)

Arthur Miller's play focusses on John Proctor (Daniel Day-Lewis) and his accuser, Abigail Williams (Winona Ryder). Hytner thinks it as timely today, amidst "rigid intellectual orthodoxies of college campuses" (p. xv), as when it was staged in 1952, in the era of McCarthyism and anticommunist witch hunts.

The Scarlet Letter (Roland Jaffe, 1995). Nathaniel Hawthorne's 1850 novel shows how the elimination of an undesirable serves to purge the eliminators of their own guilt. It also shows that stigmatizing a miscreant can strengthen social cohesion just as effectively as putting her to death. This film adaptation has a happier ending than the book. Demi Moore is Hester Prynne.

The Caine Mutiny (Columbia, Edward Dmytryk, 1954). The "tight ship"—isolated, hierarchical, vulnerable, with little room for individual rights—is the prototypical setting for elimination processes. In this case Captain Queeg (Humphrey Bogart) is eliminated. The question is how much of Queeg's lunacy is personal pathology, and how much originates in the group dynamic instigated by Fred MacMurray.

Les miserables (Columbia, 1997, Bille August). The third major film version of Victor Hugo's novel, superseding those of 1935 and 1978. Liam Neeson plays Valjean, an ex-convict in postrevolutionary France who is trying to "become honest and good again." Valjean's Chief Eliminator, Police Inspector Javert (Geoffrey Rush), devotes his life to destroying Valjean. The law is on the side of Javert.

Joan of Arc (Victor Fleming, 1948). Ingrid Bergman's portrayal of the fifteenth-century peasant girl won her an Oscar nomination. This film ably dramatizes the transition from hero to villain, the functioning of tribunals, and the social importance of humiliation. Joan confesses, then recants, much as John Proctor does three centuries later in *The Crucible*. Rome canonized her in 1920.

In the Name of the Father (1993). Based on the true story of Gerry Conlon (Daniel Day-Lewis), an Irish youth who, along with his father and aunt, is falsely charged with terrorism in London. A panic-stricken court convicts them. The son is eventually released when a determined lawyer (Emma Thompson) uncovers evidence the police had concealed.

Amadeus (Milos Forman, 1984). F. Murray Abraham won best actor for his portrayal of Salieri, a dutiful but mediocre composer upstaged by the obnoxious but more talented Mozart (Tom Hulce), and determined to get rid of him. Superb character portrayal of an ardent eliminator.

The Nasty Girl (Miramax, Michael Verhoeven, 1990). Lena Stolze plays a precocious girl who becomes the town superstar when she wins an essay prize. Then, as she uses her writing and investigative skills to dig up the town's Nazi past, she becomes a public enemy. In a threatened group, the line between hero and villain is thin. German with English subtitles.

Lord of the Flies (Harry Hook, 1990). An Americanized dramatization of William Golding's novel about 25 schoolboys lost and on their own on a tropical island after a plane crash. An autocratic leader emerges, using collective anxiety and fear to fuel a panic for bolstering his power. Group cohesion is reinforced by the group's murder of undesirables.

Lords of Discipline (Paramount, Herb Jaffe and Gabriel Katzka 1983). A story not unlike *Lord of the Flies*, but more formalized. David Keith stars as a pita-proxy among cadets in a military academy. Hard-hitting portrayal of group cohesion, mental illness, threats of publicity, a house tribunal, eliminations through varied exit-doors.

School Ties (Paramount, Stanley Jaffe and Sherry Lansing, 1992). Brendan Fraser plays a working class Jewish boy enrolled in an elite prep school on a football scholarship. Class, ethnicity and religion make him an outsider. A moment arises for the group to get rid of him. Truth is a small matter until the end.

Disclosure (Warner Bros., Barry Levinson, 1994) An exposé of jockeying for power in a large software company. Demi Moore plays an upwardly mobile executive who uses the company's sexual harassment tribunal for her advancement. Michael Douglas tries to use it to save his neck. Physical evidence helps one side win, but neither side gives up.

Oleanna (David Mamet, 1994). In this film adaptation of the controversial play, William Macy is the professor and Debra Eisenstadt the student who charges him with sexual harassment. The focus is on the relation between accuser and accused. The institution from which the accused is eliminated remains in the background.

Dead Poets Society (Peter Weir, 1989). In a traditional, button-down New England prep school, Robin Williams plays an English teacher enamoured of Whitman and Thoreau. A tragic incident demonstrates what a threat he is. An indictment with multiple signatures is arranged. Tom Schulman won an academy award for the screenplay, which includes a great send-off for the teacher.

Mr. Holland's Opus (1995). A low-brow version of *Dead Poets Society*, easier for most people to relate to. The school in this case is public, the students are from the hoi polloi, and the ostensive reason for eliminating an unbureaucratized romantic is budget cuts. Richard Dreyfuss gives an Oscar-calibre performance of the music teacher who gets sacked. Like Williams in *Dead Poets*, he gets a warm send-off from his students.

Guilty by Suspicion (Irwin Winkler, 1990). The year is 1952. Filmmaker David Merrill (Robert De Niro) has been reported to the House Un-American Activities Committee. Word has gotten around. The doors on his career are closing fast—all except the exit-door. He has only to purge himself and name his friends. Ruth Merrill (Annette Bening) stands by him. The film builds to a chilling display of the committee's hysteria in the closing scene.

Indictment: the McMartin Trial (Abby and Myra Mann, 1991). HBO dramatization of the prosecution, 1983-89, of seven staff members of a California preschool on charges of child sexual abuse. From the longest and costliest trial in U.S. history, no convictions were obtained. The film is a powerful depiction of how the mass media can fuel passions of moral panic.

A Few Good Men (Columbia, Bob Reiner, 1996). The tight ship in this case is the isolated, threatened, groupthink-saturated U.S. Naval Base at Guantanamo Bay, Cuba. An undesirable Marine is eliminated with more finality than intended. Two soldiers are on trial for the murder, but their lawyers (Tom Cruise and Demi Moore) hold the commanding officer (Jack Nicholson) responsible. From this chilling, believable portrait of despotism comes the same moral as from *Judgment at Nuremberg*.

Judgment at Nuremberg (1961). This film won Maximilian Schell an Oscar. Spencer Tracy also starred. By the time the film begins, the six million eliminations of the Holocaust are done. Having lost World War II, the Chief Eliminators have been put on trial. The question is whether their behaviour is excused by the legal pressures to which they were subject in Nazi Germany.

Black List (Telefilm Canada, 1995). A lawyer conspires with a prostitute in an extortion scheme, thereby breaking ranks with Quebec's legal-judicial elite. He is eliminated, but the real story is how the elite regroups against all odds to retain its grip on power. Michel Coté stars as the judge who defends the fraternity's integrity, and is survived by it. French with English subtitles.

River's Edge (Tim Hunter, 1987). In a clique of half a dozen teenagers estranged from the adult world, a psychopathic boy murders a girl. The film depicts in harsh, unvarnished terms how the group accepts and conceals this elimination of one of its members. Here is groupthink in the extreme, bolstered by mind-altering drugs, and exposed by an aging loner consumed by guilt for a crime of his own. Based on a true story.

Stalin (HBO, Ivan Passer, 1992). Robert Duvall plays the dictator in this biography, which shows how his frequent purges of undesirables in the party elite reinforced group solidarity and helped keep him in power. The higher the position of a newly unmasked enemy of the people, the more effectively his elimination encourages conformity. Made for TV, this three-hour film won several Golden Globe awards.

Ridicule (PolyGram Video, 1996). In prerevolutionary France, verbal and sexual weapons are deployed to humiliate a witty, civic-minded nobleman (Charles Berling), and eliminate him from the court of Louis XVI. The ending is happier for him than for the king. Oscar nominee for best foreign-language film. French with English subtitles.

Swept from the Sea (Phoenix Tristar, 1997). In a Cornish village in the late nineteenth century, the love of two pariahs (Rachel Weisz and Vincent Perez) for each other tempers the pain of exclusion. A physician (Ian McKellen) separates himself from the herd enough to embrace as his brother the stranger who comes from afar. "And bear in mind," he lectures the eliminators, "as you swill your ale and tell your filthy tales, that to take part in the violence of the mob is as low as a man who calls himself a man can fall." Yet the physician fails to recognize as his sister the stranger who is native-born. The end celebrates repentance, forgiveness, and hope.

Index